MW01597989

Breaking
Trail

MI AUG 2011

Breaking Trail

LEN MARCHAND
AND MATT HUGHES

CAITLIN PRESS INC
PRINCE GEORGE, B.C.

Copyright © Len Marchand and Matt Hughes

All rights reserved. No part of this publication may be reproduced, stored in a retrieval system or transmitted in any form, by any means without prior permission of the publisher, except by a reviewer who may quote a passage in a review.

Published by

CAITLIN PRESS Inc.
Box 23 87 Station B
Prince George BC V2N 2S6

Cover and book design by Warren Clark
Photos supplied from author's personal collection.

Canadian Cataloguing in Publication Data

Marchand, Len.
    Breaking Trail

    Includes Index
    ISBN 0-920576-80-X (bound)
    1. Marchand, Len. 2. Legislators—Canada—Biography. 3. Canada. Parliament. House of Commons—Biography. 4. Canada. Parliament. Senate—Biography. I. Hughes, Matt. II.Title.
    FC601.M3713 2000   328.71′092   C00-910023-7
    F1034.3.M367A3 2000

Caitlin Press acknowledges the financial support of Canada Council for the Arts for our publishing program. Similarly we acknowledge the support of the Arts Council of British Columbia.

Printed in Canada

THE CANADA COUNCIL | LE CONSEIL DES ARTS
FOR THE ARTS | DU CANADA
SINCE 1957 | DEPUIS 1957

I would like to dedicate this book
to my grandchildren:
Carling, Erin, Miles, Caitlin, Noah, and Keegan

Contents

Acknowledgements

B ehind every man or woman who is privileged to become a Member of Parliament stands a vast crowd of dedicated volunteers: the campaign workers who make our electoral system work. I would like to thank individually every one of the thousands of people who answered telephones, knocked on doors, stuffed envelopes and gave voters a ride to the polls, but there is not enough room to list all the names. To all of you, I want to say that you were as good a team of Liberals as any candidate ever had in his corner, and I offer once more my most sincere gratitude.

I express my special thanks to the old-timers who kept the Liberal flame flickering through the thin times and helped blow it into a bonfire when fortune turned our way: Lois Dawson, in Quesnel; Johnnie Bann and Alan Collette in Merritt; Gerard Guichon in Quilchena; Reg Small in Clearwater; Wilf Matthew in Barriere; Lloyd Askew in Salmon Arm; Stella Scallon, Speedy Field, Bill Brennan, Peter Cordonier and Gus Gottfriedson in Kamloops. I am sure there are other worthy names I have forgotten, and ask forgiveness for the holes in my memory.

I will always keep a special place in my heart for the 13,000 people of Kamloops-Cariboo who took a chance on me in the election of 1968 and made me the first Indian to be elected to the Canadian House of Commons.

I also want to thank the many people who helped put this book together: Christine Deom, for information on the Oka crisis and Iroquois history; Jim Davidson, for an early critique of the text and reminders of much from the past; Roy Derrick, for being a dedicated packrat who kept much material from the Small Business and Environment files; Sheila McCann, Mary Ellen Murdock and Karen

Nordrum, for reams of important documents from the Senate and the Library of Parliament; Bill Parchomchuk, for his excellent synopsis of the Okanagan Basin Water Study; Frances Riley, for information on the Shuswap Diversion fight and for reminding me what STRRADA stood for; Art and Shirley Hooper for reviewing the text and for background on the Maoris and New Zealand; Merv and Jean Chertkow for some old campaign memorabilia; John Leonard for a copy of the 1950s commissioner's report into the challenge to my family's Indian status; Shirley Louis, for articles from the *Vernon News*; Steve Hibbard, for information on Jack Pierce; Senate Staffers Angie Olsen, Mary Ellen McCurrach and Margaret Embleton; Russ and Helen Moses, for information on G.C. (Slim) Monture; Don Moses, for background on the Bevan and Tipperary ranches; Edward Atkinson, for information on Northwest Territories MPs; Gordon Ahenakew, Sam Sinclair, Russ Moses and Marc LeClair, for yeoman work on Aboriginal Veterans issues; my daughter Lori, my son Len Jr. and his wife Laurie, for being there with helpful hints when I needed them; and my Donna, for all her help and especially for typing notes from my truly awful handwriting.

Foreword

I hate being called an Indian. My old friend Dr. Gur Singh is an Indian—or at least he was before he became an Indo-Canadian. But I've been called—and have had to call myself—an Indian all my life, just because a certain Genoese explorer made a simple miscalculation of the circumference of the earth, five hundred years ago.

I have great respect for the peoples and ancient culture of India. But I am not an Indian. I am a *Skilwh*. That means I am a member of the Okanagan nation. But if I identify myself by that word throughout these pages, no one but my fellow Skilwh will know what I mean. And I will still have to refer to the Indian Act, and the Indian Affairs Branch (IAB), and the Department of Indian Affairs and Northern Development (DIAND), Indian Reserves and Indian Agents, because Christopher Columbus's boneheaded mistake is woven right through the history of Canada's relations with my people.

I don't like the other choices: "aboriginal person" sounds like anthropologists' jargon and is too broad a term, since it includes Inuit and Métis; "native" just means I was born here, but so were most Canadians; and "First Nations" is a pretentious, politically-loaded phrase meant to remind the rest of the population that we were here long before the first Viking longships or Basque whalers or Portuguese fishing boats bumped up against Newfoundland.

I like the way the Inuit have reclaimed their true name, doing away with "Eskimo," a derogatory term applied to them by their enemies. I like the way they have renamed their territory Nunavut, which means "Our Land" in Inuktitut. I wish we Indians could do the same. If it were up to me, I'd be called a "Dene," like many of the people of the Northwest Territories, northern Saskatchewan and northern British Columbia. It's a dignified sounding name; it's easy to say; a lot of Canadians already recognize it; and it just means "people" or "person," depending on how many you're talking about.

Maybe, a generation or two from now, we Indians will have found a name for ourselves that we can feel good about. But, for now and for clarity's sake, throughout this book I will continue to refer to myself and my people by the old, wrong word—although in my heart I am, and always will be, Skilwh.

CHAPTER I

"Hey, Indian..."

A few years ago, when David Lam was about to retire as Lieutenant Governor of British Columbia, my name was one of those tossed around in the press as a possible successor. I told Peter O'Neill of the *Vancouver Sun* that I did not want to be considered for the post and that was the end of the talk.

I could not be the representative of a hereditary monarchy. I have always believed that sovereignty rests with the people, not with one particular family—and a foreign one at that. And, although I believe the Queen does a good job as our head of state, I think that any country that still has a foreign monarch in that position has a lot more growing up to do.

If it were up to me, we'd create our Lieutenant Governors and Governors-General from amongst our own—a Nancy Greene Raine (whose sister Liz Greene worked for me in Ottawa), or a Margaret Atwood perhaps,—people who represent what is best in all of us. And even though I think the latest Governor-General, Adrienne Clarkson, is a fine choice, I'd still take that power out of the Prime Minister's hands. Instead, I'd form an electoral college from all the recipients of the Order of Canada and the Medal for Bravery—let those who have been honoured by the country for accomplishment or bravery choose a head of state we can all look up to, someone who makes us feel proud to be Canadians.

Still, to be considered as a suitable candidate to be BC's first Indian Lieutenant Governor, just as I was reaching a point in life where I was beginning to think back on where and how I had started out, brought home to me how much has changed during my lifetime. Then I got to thinking about some of the things that haven't changed, but should have. That's when I made up my mind to write this book.

I was born on November 16, 1933 at Vernon Jubilee Hospital. The town of Vernon is sixteen miles from my parents' house at Six Mile Creek on the Okanagan Reserve Number One. Since we didn't have a car until 1942 when my father bought a 1929 Plymouth four-door from my sister Josephine's boyfriend, Tim Voght, who was going off to war, my mom and dad must have hitched a ride into town, probably with my uncle Louie, who was the only one in the family who owned a car back then. I never thought to ask my parents for any such details surrounding my birth, and now it's too late.

I was the third child in a big family that mostly ran to girls. I have two older sisters, Josephine and Theresa, and four younger ones: Margaret, Joan, Pauline and Alice. A seventh girl, Martina Mary, died as an infant, and I also have a half-sister, Millie, who is my father's child from before he married my mother. It was twenty years after my birth before my parents produced my brother Raymond. By then, I had left home to get my education, so he and I never got to know each other as brothers do when they grow up together.

I didn't mind being the only boy in the household. I was well tended, and maybe even a little spoiled, as a child; my sister Josephine tells me she always used to carry me around on her back while our mother was working. And when I got big enough, I could get on a horse and go help our father with the cattle.

My dad was Joseph Marchand. He was thirty-three when I came along, a strong man, about six feet tall and weighing close to two hundred pounds in his prime, and muscled from a lifetime of hard work. He walked with a limp, though: seven years before I was born he was bucked off a horse and broke his leg in several places. The doctoring of Indians being then a somewhat chancy business, the leg never set right.

When I was young, there was a story in the family that the

Marchand name had come from a half-Indian French Canadian *coureur du bois* who had left his place as a guide on the Lewis and Clark expedition way back in the nineteenth century to marry an Okanagan woman down in what was then called the Oregon Territory. But in 1995 I asked Jean-Jacques Séguin, who lives in Hull and whose hobby is genealogical research, to cut through the legend and find the truth. He traced the family all the way back to a Normandy farm labourer, Jacques Marchand, who landed at Trois Rivieres in New France in 1656.

Mr. Séguin identified my great-grandfather, Joachim Marchand as the man who brought the name west from the Bratiscan region of Québec. He seems to have left Québec in 1840, as a young man of 24. By 1850, he was in St. Louis, Missouri, and went from there up into Montana to work for a fur company as a trader with the Blackfoot and Crow.

In 1854, he left Montana with a companion, each of them with three saddle horses, to come west into the then unsettled Washington Territory. Along the way, the horses were taken, likely by the Sioux, so the two men travelled on foot the rest of the way. Living off fish, game and berries, they followed the Missouri River to its head, then crossed the Rockies by the same pass Lewis and Clark had used, finally arriving at the Hudson's Bay fort at Kettle Falls on the Columbia River in 1855. Great-grandad Joachim squatted on a parcel of land that had fifty feet of river frontage, and took up placer mining with some success. He also married my great-grandmother, an Okanagan woman known only as Victoria. There is no record of whether they married in a church ceremony, or "after the fashion of the country," but they remained together till death did them part in 1911.

My mother was born Agnes Robinson. She was not sure who her father was: her mother, Lena Lawrence, had children with four or five men. She also had no recorded birth date, only a baptism certificate from the old church on the O'Keefe Ranch from when she was eleven years old. The old-timers used to tell me that my mother was a much sought-after beauty when she was a young woman. Boys don't recognize such things about their mothers until they grow up and see old

My father and mother, Joseph and Agnes Marchand, on their wedding day in the summer of 1925.

pictures of them. I have my parents' wedding photo, and I have to say those old-timers were right.

My mother was a devout Catholic who went to mass every chance she got. She was hard on my sisters, always keeping them on a very short rein; she was so afraid of their running around and getting pregnant. As a boy, I had more leeway—I could go to dances at the band hall or to ball games in the summer. I felt kind of bad about it, sometimes.

Neither of my parents could read or write, though my father had learned to read a little and to sign his name. During the war years, when my cousin John was overseas as a gunner in the artillery, my older sisters and I would read the newspapers to Mom and Dad, so they would know what he was involved in. My sisters and I had been to school, and though I am now ashamed to admit it, I used to tease our mother sometimes when we went to the grocery store in town, pointing to signs and labels and asking her, "What does that say, Mom?" or, "What size is that tin?" But although my mother was not educated, she was an intelligent woman, and would manage to do her shopping even without help from her smart-alec son.

Later on, when I could call myself educated, I would think back on how it was for my parents, how they had to live in a tightly circumscribed world because they could not read, and I would feel an overwhelming sadness and a strong tinge of guilt. When I was in the Senate, and Joyce Fairbairn tried to get me involved in her literacy programs, I'd always beg off; I couldn't bring myself to do more than cheer her on from the sidelines. The memories hurt too much.

We were farmers and cattle ranchers in a very small way: subsistence agriculture is the anthropologists' term. My parents supplemented our farm income any way they could. Dad would sometimes go off the reserve to a logging camp for a week at a time, and Mom and the rest of us worked for the Chinese truck gardeners who leased land on the reserve. My first job was pulling weeds and thinning onions and so on for fifteen cents an hour. The mixed hay and alfalfa that we grew on twenty acres on the other side of Six Mile Creek went to feed our own stock—usually thirty to forty head of mixed cattle that we would sell to a stock dealer who sold them on to feed lots in Alberta—as well as the work and saddle horses that were needed to run the ranch.

When I was little, we lived in a small house, maybe sixteen by twenty feet with a tiny attic. It had rough planking on the outside and the interior walls were covered in shiplap and cheap, unpatterned wallpaper. Grandpa Louie Marchand had separated from Grandma Mary Anne, and came to live in a lean-to addition on the back of the house. One February morning in 1941, Grandpa left the dampers too wide open on his pot-bellied stove when he came to eat with us, and the whole place caught on fire. The wood was dry so it went up fast, filling the little space with smoke and flames. My parents rushed the five of us kids out into the air, and for a few moments there was near-panic until we located my two-year-old sister Joan. There was no fire department, and the creek was too far away to form a bucket brigade, even if we'd had buckets. The house burned to the ground, and we lost everything we had.

Our next house was not much bigger—fourteen by twenty-four feet—heated by a wood-burning stove and lit by oil and gas lamps. It had one bedroom, but later on my parents added a sixteen-by-fourteen foot kitchen, and still later, another fourteen-by-twenty-four-foot extension. Out back was a corral and a hay barn, and a two-hole privy. When I was growing up on the rez, I would have had to walk for four hours to see an electric light or a tap you just had to turn to get water. Sometimes, when we went to town for supplies, my parents would buy us kids a couple of bricks of ice cream; but we had to hurry home to eat it before it melted, because there was no way to keep it frozen.

My mother would scrub our clothes on an old washboard in a steel tub outside. We'd haul buckets of water up from Six Mile Creek, and light a fire under the washtub. We were up with the sun to do the chores, and when the daylight went, the day was over. We lived like the pioneer families that today's kids read about in history books: except that we weren't newcomers to this land; we had always been here.

Some years, instead of putting in hay, my dad would rent out our land to the Chinese gardeners; at $35 to $40 an acre for the season, the proceeds represented a substantial part of the family income. My dad would also hire himself out to plough for the gardeners—they usually preferred soil that had been turned over by a horsedrawn plough because it was not compacted the way it would be if a tractor had been over it.

As a small boy, I went everywhere with my father, riding behind him on his horse, but it was my Grandpa Louie who taught me how to ride on his placid, patient cayuse, Ol' Bawley. My grandfather knew everything when I was little. He could speak French as well as English and Okanagan. He would take me out grouse hunting, or we'd just go riding aimlessly, and he would tell me old tales and all kinds of fascinating lore about the woods and the animals.

Once I could ride, I spent as much time as I could in the saddle. By my teens, I was a genuine cowboy, and I loved the work. With my dad or on my own, I rode the range and did all the things that come with looking after cattle: roping, branding, vaccinating, castrating. We'd make sure they got into the right places to graze, kept them off the open highways—there were no fences back then—and herded

On Ol' Bawley, Grandpa Louie's horse, near the Old Six Mile School, with Charlie Curteis, son of my first teacher, Tom Curteis, in the late spring of 1939. My Dad and I rode down for a visit.

them in when it was time to feed them for the winter. I learned to sit a saddle as if I had been born there, and I could even do a few rope tricks.

I was at home on the range. I fitted into the landscape in a way that I can't describe. I was happy; I didn't think about it then, but if I'd had to, I would have said that I was where I was supposed to be. It never occurred to me, then, that there was anywhere else to be. I assumed that I would be a farmer and a cattleman like my dad—only I would first learn more about the white man's way of doing things. Because, there was no question then, the white man's way was the right way.

Nowadays, when my people's pride and our sense of identity have been reborn, it is probably difficult for young Indian men and women to understand how it was for my parents' generation. For them, to be Indian was to feel inferior. Nobody had to stand on a street corner and lecture us on it—it was self-evident. The whites had nice homes; we had lousy homes. They had good clothes; we had crummy clothes. They had new cars; we had jalopies.

It wasn't that the whites were inherently better than us. But their *ways* were superior. They were better educated, knew more. That's why they were the doctors, the teachers, the storekeepers, the Indian agents. When I was growing up, and my parents were showing me how to do things right, they would say, "This is how a white man would do it." I can hear my father's voice saying it now, "This is how a white man would" do this or that. We heard it over and over again. It was drilled into us.

It was possible to learn the white man's superior ways. You did that by going to the white man's school, which in my childhood, was a quarter of a mile down the dirt road from our house at Six Mile Creek. It was a white, wood-framed, single-roomed school house, the kind you would have found throughout rural Canada in the 1930s, with wood and cast-iron desks bolted together in rows, and a pot-bellied stove for winter heat. It offered grades one through six when I started, and was operated by the Indian Affairs Branch. I first went to school as an unofficial accompaniment to my older sisters. I'd have been three or four then; when my parents were working, there'd be no one to look after me, so they let me tag along rather than keep Josephine or Theresa at home, missing school to mind me. I don't recall that I made any particular impression on the academic world at that stage of my education, but by the time I was six and could begin grade one, I was hungry to learn.

My teacher for the first three grades was Tom Curteis, a kindly-natured white man with a wife and two small children of his own. I was lucky to begin with such a dedicated educator. He pushed me as fast as I could go, challenged me to reach further and grab more, and I reached and grabbed for everything he put in my way. Before I finished the first year, he had me reading at a grade three level, and I was winning spelling bees.

After three years, he moved on and later became principal of a large elementary school in Victoria. By the time I was in university, he came back to the rez with his family for a visit. He said that he had been keeping an eye on my career, such as it was at that point, and that he had always believed that Theresa and I could have gone however far we wanted to. Theresa was the brightest of us all, but she didn't get the chance I got: she worked picking tomatoes and pulling weeds in the Chinese gardens and later was a housemaid for a Kamloops doctor.

After Tom Curteis there were a few other teachers through grades four through six, who did not make much of an impression on me. Then came Sister Patricia, a Franciscan nun who had previously taught at an Indian school in Ontario. I know that at some reserve and residential schools, a lot more emphasis was put on saving our souls than on developing our minds. But Sister Patricia made no bones about it: she was there to educate us, and she expected us to learn. On her first day, she told us she meant to work us hard, and that we would have to meet her high standards. She held up a scribbler, and said, "This is the kind of sloppy work I don't want to see any more of." Of course, it was mine—I could read and spell just about anything, but my handwriting, then and now, was awful.

Grades seven and eight were being taught at the little school on our reserve by the time I finished grade six, so I didn't have to go off to the residential school, seventy miles away in Kamloops at the age of 12. That left two more years for Sister Patricia to pound away at four of us in the upper grades whom she had singled out for extra attention: Murray Alexis, Lloyd Wilson, Jim Cameron and me. Sister Patricia helped us prepare to write province-wide exams based on the provincial curriculum, spending many summer evenings taking us through Robert Louis Stevenson's *Kidnapped* on her back porch.

Ours was not strictly a church school, but we were a Catholic reserve and the priests had great influence, so all of our teachers were Catholic. We had no community centre or even a grocery store on the rez in those days, and although people would sometimes hold dances in their houses if they had a big enough room, the church was the only real social focus in the community. The old religion, from before the missionaries arrived, was almost all forgotten by my parents' generation. We still referred to the Creator, *Koolenchooten*, and remembered that Coyote was his messenger. And I recall that the old-timers had their songs; they'd beat the drum and chant on certain occasions. But all our prayers were translations of the Our Father and the Hail Mary into Okanagan—except for some hymns sung over the dead. At funerals, people still said the old words.

Okanagan is in some ways a more complicated language than English. It makes narrower distinctions in some respects. For example, English distinguishes between siblings to the extent of identifying brothers and sisters; Okanagan has separate words for older brother and younger brother, and for older sister and younger sister. We always called my mother's mother *Tumma*, the Okanagan word for maternal grandmother; my father's mother would have been *Kukna*, but for some reason we always called her by the English word Gramma.

Gramma's name was Mary Anne Marchand. She used to lead the prayers at all the funerals, and when she died in 1958, my father took her place. He was reluctant to accept the role, but people expected it of him because he was an authority on the Okanagan language. He knew all the words to the prayers and the old names for plants and animals. "If Joe doesn't know it," people would say, "nobody knows it."

Dad didn't think much of the old spiritual ways. He didn't believe that the "Indian doctors," as we called them, had any special powers to curse or to cure. "You can't change people's lives by dancing and blowing smoke around," he told me. But Gramma prepared medicines from plants the way the old people used to. She'd mix pine resin with axle grease and make a poultice to put on cuts and scrapes, or chew up wild rose leaves to put on a bee sting. I still do that, myself— it cancels the stinging right away. When my mother was dying from colonic cancer, she would make a tea from twigs of the saskatoon berry bush; it seemed to give her comfort.

Both of my parents were quite intelligent people. If they were young today, they would be getting an education. But they were born into a generation that was still culture-shocked from contact with the whites. So they did the best they could with what they had. They never really knew what education was. Even when I came back from university to join the scientific staff at the Kamloops agricultural research station, my mom and dad weren't all that clear about what a university degree was. But they always knew they wanted me to be educated.

～～～～

That was why when I was fifteen, they went with me one September morning in 1949, out to the dirt road by the bad smelling lake on the O'Keefe Ranch to get on a cattle truck that would take me to the residential school. It was a warm day, clear and bright the way it usually is in late summer in the Okanagan Valley.

We waited within sight of the old church where my mother had been baptized until the truck came up the road from the south. It had started out in Oliver, stopping in Penticton and Westbank to pick up students for the Kamloops Indian Residential School. I said goodbye to my mom and dad and climbed into the truck with my suitcase. I held onto the truck's side rack and watched for a while as my parents dwindled in size behind me.

It didn't occur to me to think then that the school ought to have had a bus to pick us up, instead of a cattle truck. Kamloops Indian Residential School (KIRS) owned a truck because the school had valuable beef and dairy herds. The cattle were tended by the students under the direction of priests and lay workers.

Nowadays, there are two-and four-lane highways between Kamloops and Vernon, and it's an easy trip along the blacktop, not much more than an hour. In 1949, it was two hours of dust and bumps. But I didn't mind. I was meeting new people, Indian boys and girls like me, and some of them would become lifelong friends.

More important, it was my choice to go. I hadn't been pulled away from my family at the age of five or six and shipped off to be "civilized." I'd had a good childhood with a loving family, and I could have stayed with them on the reserve—farming a little, tending the cattle, riding my horse—but I wanted to be *more* than I was. If I'd given up on education, as most young Indians of my generation did long before they finished elementary school, the only goal I could have set would have been to help dad increase the farm. And that would have been hard to do on a small reserve of twenty-five thousand acres that, even then, supported about four hundred people. Twenty-five thousand acres may sound like a lot to city dwellers (the average urban lot is about one-quarter of an acre), but in cattle country it's enough for only a small ranch.

I was an adventuresome boy. I didn't duck my head and back down from a challenge, and if wanting to develop my brains instead of my muscles meant leaving home, then I would do it.

We arrived at Kamloops Indian Residential School in the afternoon. To me, it was an imposing building: three stories of red brick on a stone foundation, with barns and corrals out back. We jumped off the truck, and the staff—most of them priests and nuns—divided us by gender and marched us into the separate wings of the school; boys and girls did not mix at KIRS, except in classrooms and chapel.

We boys were arranged in single file and marched down into the basement by a kindly man named Brother O'Brien. We were to take a shower, he said; I didn't mind, my face and hair were pretty dusty from the trip. Then he told us we also had to wash our hair in coal oil, "to kill any lice."

I was a little upset. We were clean people; my mother would have been horrified if there had ever been a louse in our house. I thought to myself, *Is this the way we're going to be treated? Is this the way they treat Indians here?*

I said, "I'm not lousy," but Brother O'Brien had heard all the protestations a hundred times. He handed out the coal oil, and he didn't look like the kind of man who welcomed an argument. Besides, he was white, and we were Indian—we did what we were told.

When we were clean, they showed us to our dormitory on the top floor. It was a long, narrow room, with beds on either side, and plenty of light from the tall windows that overlooked the barns. They gave us time to put our things away; then it was back down the stairs to the basement and get in line to enter the dining hall for supper.

We ate at long tables that seated seven or eight to a side. No talking, no horseplay, we were warned: eating was a serious business. The food was a disappointment: watery potatoes and over-boiled vegetables that my mom would have been ashamed to offer us. There were 350 head of good Herefords out on the range, but none of that beef was finding its way into the kids. I was already missing the pies and cakes my big sisters used to bake. But there was plenty of milk and butter from the dairy herd, and slabs of good bread. I soon learned that the thickness of your slice was a status symbol. A thicker crust meant you had a girlfriend who was a big wheel in the kitchen.

My days at Kamloops Indian Residential School soon fell into a regular routine. At 5:30 a.m., Peter Secora, a big, strong growly man who was the farm foreman, clumped through the dormitory, deliberately thumping the heels of his boots loudly on the floor. That was our alarm clock. Any boy who wasn't up before Peter reached his bed would feel a yank on his toes. If anyone stayed in bed so long that the foreman had to make a second pass, he would overturn the bed, dumping the late riser onto the floor.

We'd dress quickly, then head for our lockers in the basement, pull on boots, caps and coats, and trail Peter out to the barn for early milking. The barn was spotless, with 30 head of first-rate Holsteins waiting for us in their milking stanchions. There were none of the electric pumps you see in modern dairy barns: we washed the animals' teats and sat down to milk them by hand. My cow was named

Nora; she was easy to milk, although she had lost one teat to mastitis. I'd worked with cows before, but with Nora I improved my skills until I could get the milk out of her so fast the foam would flow over the rim of the pail.

After milking, it was back to the chapel in the school for prayers and hymns or sometimes an early mass. Then, finally, we'd get breakfast, which was always the worst meal of the day: lumpy rolled oats or thin cream of wheat, made even less appetizing because we could smell the bacon and eggs that the staff were having next door. I used to long to be at home, biting into a slice of the fried bread we called *sun-cha-chiwhula*—bannock bread in English—delicious hot from the pan with jam or a slice of baloney on top.

We'd get through breakfast as quickly as we could, then go on to morning classes. One thing I have to say for that residential school: even though we worked weekends and some half-days during the week, digging potatoes and pulling turnips, the staff did put a definite priority on giving us an education. The classrooms were big, well-lit rooms, with desks as modern as any you could have found on the west side of Vancouver in 1949.

And the teachers were just as good. Two of the best I ever knew were Sister Anne Mary, who taught us French, math and biology, and Sister Mary Antonius, our history and English instructor. I've heard tales about nuns in residential schools who were more interested in seeing that the Indian children under their command learned discipline—something else we were supposed to lack—than in filling their heads with knowledge. But Sisters Anne Mary and Mary Antonius were of a different breed—they taught as if they expected us to learn, and most of us responded.

I got good marks, sometimes in friendly competition with two other students: Robert LeCamp, a very bright guy from Kamloops who had the most perfect, precise handwriting I ever saw; and Rose Terry from Bridge River. Each of us continually tried to beat the others and be top student in grade nine.

I have never thought of myself as particularly bright, although I suppose I must have a few brains because learning has always been a pretty painless experience for me. I liked school, and I worked hard at it; the more schooling I got, the harder I worked. Sometimes I would think to myself, *I'm working hard so that when I go back to the reserve I will make a better life for myself and my family.* But most of the time, I just enjoyed learning for its own sake. Somewhere along the way, though, another motivation took root in the back of mind: that somehow, by getting educated, I would be able to do something to help my people. I don't remember the first time that idea came to me, but it probably sprouted sometime during the year that I spent at Kamloops Indian Residential School.

Of course, it wasn't all praying, field work and classroom instruction. We played a lot of sports—baseball, basketball and hockey, none of which I was much good at—and we had some fine athletes. Probably the most outstanding was Joe Stanley Michel, who now lives in Chase: I once saw him score 60 points in a basketball game. He was also the first high school graduate from KIRS in 1952.

A select few of us who knew cattle well would also be taken by Father O'Grady to show the school's prize Holsteins at the Armstrong Fair. The school always came back with blue ribbons: those cows were well looked after. On the way down to the fair in 1949, I went with a half dozen of the other boys in the priest's brand new stretched Dodge. It was a real excursion for all of us, and we got a little happy, the way teenagers will, making jokes and singing. Father O'Grady pulled over to the side of the road and gave us a lecture, then led us all in the rosary. The discipline of the church was never far away.

Sister Anne Mary taught us to sing as a choir, and she knew what she was doing. Being a nun, she'd had a lifetime's exposure to choral music, I suppose, and she applied all her experience to making us sound good. The result was that KIRS had a superb choir; we always cleaned up at the annual local music festival. The year that I was there, I was half the tenor section. The other half was a boy named Nelson Edwards from Pavilion. Sister Anne Mary was always urging Nelson and me to raise our volume a little because though we won in our category, the judges' critique said, "We would have liked to have heard a little more from the tenors." If any of those judges are reading this, I want to assure them that Nelson and I were giving it all we had.

The reader might be expecting me to tell a few horror stories about physical and sexual abuse at the residential school. But I know of no incidences at KIRS. There was the strap for serious transgressions, to be sure, but that was no different from the corporal punishment that was doled out in those days to white students in the better schools of Vancouver and Victoria. I was never abused, and I never heard of anyone else who was mistreated at the Kamloops school. The nuns and priests and brothers had some old-fashioned notions about what Indians were and what we needed, notions that today's young Indians would probably find at best quaint, and at worst, offensive. But they meant well by us, they genuinely cared about us, and they all did their duty by us as they saw fit.

But, all in all, I would rather have been with my family. Though I had made good friends, I was lonesome for my parents and sisters all through that year. So I was very glad when it turned out that the Indian Affairs Branch would pay for me to room and board in Vernon, and that I could attend the high school there. This was quite a big deal at the time. It had only recently become legal for Indians to

With my father and brother, Ray, at Six Mile Creek in the summer of 1962. I was helping to break in another saddle horse.

attend public schools; ordinarily, we were handed over to the churches under the authority of the Indian Act. I was the first of my people ever to enrol in Vernon High School.

It was Ron Sampson, the Indian Agent, who fixed it. And maybe it's time to say a few words about what an Indian Agent was in those times: He was "the be-all and the end-all" for Indians on the reserves. He was Mister Everything. All of our lives were funnelled up to the Indian Agent. We might propose, but he disposed. Somewhere up above him were layers of district supervisors and regional directors, all the way to the deputy minister and the Minister of Citizenship and Immigration in Ottawa; we knew nothing of them—we knew the Indian Agent, and what he said decided how we lived.

He was in an office, sixteen miles away in Vernon. He did not come to us; we went to him. There was a band council that met to vote on resolutions, but the resolutions were worded by the Indian Agent and brought to the council meeting pretyped with the spaces marked with x's for the councillors' signatures. He was the authority under the Indian Act, and the Indian Act governed almost every important aspect of our lives; what the Act didn't control, the church did.

Under the Indian Act, we had to live on reserves. We couldn't vote, couldn't buy a bottle of beer. We couldn't sell or lease our land without the Indian Agent's permission. If the reserve earned any money, the band council had no right to decide what to do with it; they couldn't write a cheque or take out a loan. Only the Indian Agent could do that for us. We were not "persons" under the laws of Canada or British Columbia—unless we broke one of them.

Still, I have to thank Ron Sampson for making it possible for me to leave the Kamloops school and come home—or at least within visiting distance of home. The Indian Affairs Branch paid for me to board with a family of Ukrainian-Canadians, Tom and Mary Ewanchuk. They had a small holding with an orchard and pasture enough for a milk cow in then rural South Vernon. They were good-hearted people, salt of the earth. I had only one disappointment when my dad drove me over to get acquainted: after the months away at KIRS, I had been hoping that the Ewanchuks would have a bathroom—I expected a white family to have all the conveniences we lacked—but in those days there were plenty of farm families still waiting for indoor plumbing, and Tom and Mary were among them. Modern Canadians, who have encountered outhouses only in parks and campsites while on summer vacation, may think that outdoor facilities are not much of an ordeal. I can only suggest that they try one on a cold, rainy February night with the wind blowing sleet through the chinks in the door, while their bodies are playing host to a flu virus.

The Ewanchuks were the first white people I'd ever known informally, but I didn't go through much of a culture shock. I settled in to their spare room—the first time I'd ever had a room all to myself—and soon it was pretty much like living at home, except there was a little more space. The big difference was the food: Mary Ewanchuk cooked things I'd never heard of—*peroheh, borscht, notchenka*—and she started me on a long-running addiction to Ukrainian cuisine.

The day after Labour Day in 1950, Dad drove me in to Vernon. We walked up the steps on the southeast side of the big high school and went into the wide hallway near the administration office. I was looking around, curious to see how much different this place would be from the residential school. Not much, was my first reaction: there were the same kinds of cups in the trophies case and the same smell of chalk dust and floor cleaner. The only real difference was that there were no crucifixes or cassocks, and the picture on the wall was of King George VI instead of Jesus. I didn't notice my father's reaction; it didn't occur to me until much later that this must have been a wholly new experience for him—he had never set foot in a high school before.

I was looking my best; I wasn't conscious that I was in any way representing my people, but I wanted to look good for my own sake. I had on my best dress pants, a new jacket, thoroughly shined shoes and a green felt fedora. The hat occasioned my only moment of deep alienation from the all-white student body—I was the only boy in school who was wearing one. Indian kids were not on the same fashion track as whites. I took it off and wished I had somewhere to hide it.

But that was it—no taunts, no bullying, no tap on the shoulder followed by, "What the hell are you doing here, Indian?" Some people stared; I probably stared back. You have to remember that, although we lived only a few miles apart and went to the same grocery stores and movie theatres on Saturday afternoon, Indians and whites lived an entirely separate existence in those days. It was like the African herds in those nature documentaries David Suzuki used to present on the CBC: the wildebeests and zebras travel and graze side by side, but they might as well be on different continents.

I was sixteen years of age, and had lived all my life in a country where whites were the overwhelming majority, but I knew only one white kid to talk to. His name was Ed Yawney, and his father ran the second-hand store in Vernon where we used to buy our coal oil and high-test gas for our lamps and lanterns. Ed was a year or two ahead of me at Vernon High; he took me under his wing when I started school, and showed me a few of the ropes. I soon made other friends, and after a few months I fitted in. I was not the lonely little Indian I had worried about being.

I settled in and went to work: five days a week I went to school; weekends and holidays were for family. In the summers I helped my dad, haying and cow-punching, or my mom and sisters in the vegetable gardens. I was learning how to be a farmer, because the school—in consultation with the Indian Agent, but not with me or my family—had enrolled me in the new vocational agriculture program that had just started up.

It was a happy time for me. I felt that what I was learning in school would be useful for my family. It was pretty easy, so I was getting good marks, and I enjoyed being with my family when school was out. When my dad and I were out on the range, we didn't spend all our time working; there was a special patch of flat ground where we used to race our horses. He used to ride my sister's young horse, a gelding named Bob. And I would ride my mare, Trigger.

She was a fast and feisty half-thoroughbred that I named after Roy Rogers' palomino in the movies. I bought her from my cousin Emery Louis for twenty dollars—he'd picked her up in a sale, but hadn't had time to break her—and my father and I set ourselves to make a good saddle horse out of her. The trouble was, she must have been teased by a previous owner because she had picked up a bad habit of kicking at anybody who came too close.

Our first efforts at convincing her to let me sit on her back were pretty sad. So one evening Dad and I decided it was now or never. We tied her closely to a tree and three-legged her: that means we put a rope around her neck and then over her left hind leg to pull it up off the ground, so she couldn't move. We saddled her up, then my father maneuvered his horse in close to her, with me sitting behind his saddle. I slid over onto Trigger. We gave her back the use of all four legs, but Dad had wrapped her halter rope around his saddle horn, so she was snubbed up tight against his horse. Then we rode pretty hard and fast around the hills, the two horses still tight together, until she was tired and lathered.

After two or three hours, Trigger was settled down and responding well, so we headed for home. Not far from our house, we came to a narrow part of the trail where we couldn't ride two abreast. My father eased off on my mare's halter rope, so I could fall in behind him. Two seconds later, I was on the ground with a black eye and a skinned elbow. But I got right back on and rode her around for another hour or so. From then on she and I were good friends. Of all the horses I had when I was growing up, she was the best; and the night Dad and I broke her is still a special memory of my time with him.

A funny thing happened to me on the way to grade twelve: somewhere along the way I stopped thinking that I would finish high school and stay on the reserve to farm with my dad. As I went up through the grades, I acquired a desire to be educated. At first, I didn't really know what a university was, or even exactly where it was, but gradually I discovered that I wanted to go there. The trouble was: when I finished grade twelve, I found that my vocational agriculture program was a dead end; after three years of work, I had none of the academic credits required for university admission. I had nothing.

There had been an automatic assumption on everybody's part, that there was no point in streaming an Indian kid through the general academic curriculum. The Indian Agent and the school authorities, in their wisdom, had plunked me down in a blind-alley program. This was not active discrimination on anybody's part; it was systemic, unthinking, and natural to the Canada of 1954. After all, who had ever heard of Indians getting university degrees? The powers that were in those days would no more have thought of preparing a teenage girl to enter engineering school.

Fortunately for me, there were some people willing and able to think new thoughts. The man who taught my agriculture courses, Norman Galloway, and the Vernon High School boys' counsellor, A.N. (Al) Humphries, got me to take another year of high school. I took all of my academic prerequisites—chemistry, biology, French, English and two years worth of math—in one year, then went on to grade thirteen. I came out of it with enough credits to enter as a second-year student at the University of British Columbia's agriculture faculty.

So in September, 1955, I boarded a Greyhound at the Vernon bus depot and went south to Vancouver for the first time. When I got off, I was in downtown Vancouver at the bus station across the street from the old British Columbia Regiment Headquarters. I took a cab to a house on West Fifteenth Avenue near Cambie, the home of Sam and Ruby Smythe, where Indian Affairs had arranged for me to board. Sam was a Scotsman who had come to Canada forty years before and had worked as an expert concrete finisher around Vancouver. Ruby was a kind of mom-away-from-mom to me and a group of Indian girls who were training to be nurses.

All of our expenses were paid directly by the Indian Affairs Branch. None of us ever handled a penny of the money. At the time, that didn't bother me at all: I had come from a small world in which the Indian Agent was, if not God himself, a very close second. We were used to having our responsibilities taken over by outside forces. Later on, when I was an assistant to the federal Minister of Indian Affairs, I worked to change things so that adult Indians in school were able to handle their own finances. But in the fall of 1955 at the age of 22, all that mattered to me was that, at last, I was at university. I was completely happy.

I hadn't been there long before I was invited to attend a reception for new students at Dean Blythe Eagles' home in an upscale neighbourhood in suburban Burnaby. It was a beautiful house with a view overlooking Deer Lake. The president of UBC, Norman Mackenzie, came and spoke to us, welcomed us to the university. I suppose it was just a nice little event for most of the students, but for me, an Indian off the reserve at Six Mile Creek, it was a significant moment. I was standing in an elegant room, among some important people—white people—everybody talking in quiet voices and sipping coffee and tea from fine china, and nobody looked at me as if I had just arrived from Mars. I realized that I was there, like everybody else in that room, because I deserved to be—I had earned my place at UBC.

And I made the most of it. Father O'Grady and the nuns at the residential school would probably have congratulated themselves on a job well done. I was one hard-working Indian student. I had enrolled in the Faculty of Agriculture, but I soon put behind me any thoughts about turning myself into a better farmer. Instead, I found myself embroiled in a love affair with plant sciences. It was pure fascination—the more I learned, the more I wanted to know.

At the same time, as I spent more and more time in the company of whites—there weren't many Indians to socialize with at UBC—I knew that I wanted to do something for my people. It had become clear to me that, given the same chances and opportunities that whites enjoyed, we could do anything anybody else could do and do it just as well. Today's young Indians, reading what I've just written, would probably say something like, "Well, duh...," because it's so obvious that the most crucial difference between haves and have-nots in any society is the degree of opportunity—especially the opportunity to be educated. But I came up from a world in which equality was anything but obvious. For me and my generation, the journey toward understanding that we were just as good as anybody else was a mountain that we had to climb, step by step.

I worked hard at university, but it wasn't just because I felt obligated to do my best—it was fun to learn. Also, because all my funds were funnelled through Indian Affairs, I never had much money to do much else. The big social event of the agriculture faculty was the annual ball, known all over campus as the Farmers' Frolic, at the old UBC armory. By the time I was in my last year at UBC, the Aggie Ball had evolved into a semi-formal affair with a fancy orchestra; in my first year, however, the dance still retained its original rural feel—it was a great, big, down-home, country-style square dance. And because I'd had some experience in the art, I was the man at the microphone, alternating with another student named Ross Husdon, calling the do-se-do's and allemands.

I kept in touch with home. My parents had no phone, but I wrote to my sister Theresa, and she wrote back on my parents' behalf. At Christmas 1955, I got on the bus and went home, and slipped easily back into the kind of life I had always known, being with my family, feeding cows and cutting wood. I found that I could be comfortable in both the little world of the reserve, sitting around talking about crops and cattle and kids, and in the wider world that intersected at the university, going out for a beer with my fellow "Aggies," talking politics and science.

But, every now and then, I would be reminded that I was not just another student. There was a whole set of laws that applied to me that didn't apply to my white friends. One of those occasions was the time I broke the law to get a bottle of whisky.

It was after Christmas of 1958. I had been home to see my family, but then I came back to school early because I had a pile of work to finish up at UBC. I thought it would be nice to have a drink to celebrate the holidays. My friends were all away, so I went into the provincial government liquor store on West Broadway.

In those puritanical days, all the liquor was safely behind a counter guarded by a clerk—no open shelves and shopping carts. You lined up, asked the clerk for what you wanted and waited while he went into the back to get it. I got into line. It being Christmas, there were quite a few people ahead of me. Vancouver wasn't as multi-ethnic then as it is now, but there was still a variety of colours in the queue.

I had been nervous before I walked into the store. But as the line moved slowly forward, I started to sweat. I was sure that when it came to be my turn, the clerk would look at me and say, "Hey, Indian, you have no right to be here." I wanted to slink out, but I also wanted to be like anybody else, to be able to buy a bottle and drink a toast to the season.

I resolved that, if the clerk refused to serve me, I would tell him I was Chinese. I had occasionally been mistaken for a Chinese Canadian since coming to the city. It bothered me that I was planning to lie; I had been raised to tell the truth and take the consequences. It didn't occur to me then that I was preparing to deny my heritage—that realization came later. But I did know that I was breaking the law, and even though it was a law I didn't agree with, a law that was patently unjust, the idea of breaking the law was no small matter to me.

But when I got to the counter, the clerk just glanced at me and said, "What'll it be?"

"A 26-er of Hudson Bay rye," I said.

He wrapped it up, I paid the price, and walked out into the December cold with sweat running down my back. I never bought another bottle of booze until that law was repealed in the summer of 1960.

In my last year at high school, I had worked in a sawmill near Vernon, and when UBC broke for the summer of 1956, I went back to hauling lumber off the green chain and tending the big slasher saw that chopped up waste before it was sent to the beehive burner. Maybe I had gotten just a little soft, living the student's life, but after a couple of days on the green chain, I had blisters on my toes and fingers. When I heard there was a summer job open at the Canadian Department of Agriculture's Kamloops research station, I went for it. I didn't realize it at the time, but that summer job was the beginning of a long and happy association with the scientists who conducted the station's research program.

Neither did the scientists, apparently, because they started me out as a farm labourer—mainly because I knew how to drive a tractor.

I lived in the bunkhouse and spent my days doing farm chores and moving irrigation pipe until somebody found a use for me as a technician on various experiments.

The researchers—Bill Hubbard, Alastair McLean, Bill Pringle, Hugh Nicholson and Al Van Ryswyk—each had different projects on the go, all related to the cattle industry. I spent a lot of time out in the field, cutting alfalfa—each variety growing in its own plot—and collecting range plant specimens. I worked mostly with Bill Hubbard and Al McLean, both of whom had masters degrees in range management, and I began to be quite enamoured of range sciences.

In the fall of 1956, I went back to Sam and Ruby Smythe and another term at UBC, convinced that I wanted to be a range management scientist. The months at the Kamloops station had shown me what research was, and I wanted more of it. I concentrated my studies on plant sciences—anatomy, physiology, genetics—with sidelines into related subjects like zoology. Back then, probably not more than one in a thousand people could define the word "ecologist", but that's what I was set on becoming. By the summer of 1957, I was back at the Kamloops station again, only this time there were no farm chores; I was a full-time research technician, and the work was even more absorbing.

In the next year at university, I finished all the required courses for a Bachelor of Science degree, except for my deficiency in math, which had been niggling at my conscience ever since high school. I had flunked first-year math at UBC, then put it out of my mind while I indulged my fascination with plant sciences. Eventually, I would go back to summer school in 1959, retake the math course and ace it.

In the summer of 1958, I took a job at another Department of Agriculture research station further up country in Smithers, a small town dependent on the forest resource northwest of Prince George. Premier W.A.C. Bennett's program to open up the province's Interior with highways and rail lines hadn't yet hit its stride, and Smithers was about as remote a place as British Columbia offered. The work was different, too: I spent the summer working on weed control experiments.

A number of things happened to me in 1958 that I won't forget.

For one thing, I experienced overt discrimination for the first time, at the hands of the Indian Affairs Branch. Now, some readers may be surprised that I had lived almost twenty-five years without feeling the pain of active racial discrimination. Sure, there were obvious biases that were built into the system: I couldn't vote; when I wanted a bottle of rye to take to a university dance, I had to ask one of my white friends to get it for me. But it wasn't until 1958 that anyone ever decided that I couldn't have a job I was well qualified for because I was an Indian.

I had heard that there was an opening for an Assistant Superintendent—that's what they were calling Indian Agents then—at the Kamloops Indian Agency. I applied for the job, and when the time came for an interview, I went down from Smithers to Vancouver. To my knowledge, I was the only applicant with a university degree—there certainly weren't many people with degrees in Indian Agencies in those days. And I was sure as hell the only one with a lifetime's experience of the system. But the job went to a white war veteran; I came in sixth.

There is no doubt in my mind that I was the best qualified applicant for that job. And there is no doubt in my mind that I would have got the job if I had been white. It was direct discrimination against me because of my race, and it hurt. For a moment, everything that I had achieved in life—my marks, my university credits, my degree—was cancelled out. For that moment, I was just an Indian, being treated the way Indians were always treated, but then the moment passed, and I was mad. Remembering it today, I'm still mad.

There was another incident that got under my skin, only this time the prejudice came from my side of the division between Indians and the rest of the world. I was at my parents' home when a neighbour—like most people on the reserve, she was also a relative—came to visit. I was telling her about how I had got my degree, and feeling pretty pleased about it.

The neighbour waved her hand and said, "Oh, they just took pity on a little Indian. You'll never get a job anyway."

It reminded me of a story that an old friend used to tell, about a lobsterman who was coming back from the dock with two buckets of lobsters, and the crustaceans were trying to get out. When he got home, he found that one of the buckets was empty, while the other one was still full of squirming lobsters.

His wife asked him how come the lobsters from one bucket had got away, while the others hadn't.

"Well," he said, pointing to the full bucket, "these are Indian lobsters. As soon as they saw one of their neighbors about to get out of the bucket, they all dragged him back in."

So, after experiencing two different flavours of racism, one from Indian Affairs and another from one of my own relatives, it was no accident that 1958 found me ready to do more than wonder how I might help my people. I was determined to get involved. I would make some changes happen. So I joined the North American Indian Brotherhood (NAIB).

I had been thinking about it for a while. The NAIB's president was George Manuel, of the Neskonlith band of the Shuswap people. I used to see him sometimes at the baseball games that were always a big draw on the reserves. He was interested in me because, as an educated Indian, I was a rarity; I was interested in him because he was a leader and a fighter.

I became active in the NAIB in the fall of 1958, after moving back down to Kamloops to work as a technician at the Department of Agriculture station. During the week, I was busy at the station. Weekends, I was out talking to my people about the value of education, one of the key issues on the organization's agenda. I also acted as a note-taker, chauffeur and general go,-for. I drove George all over the place, and the talks we had about our people's situation added a whole new layer to my education.

In the late 1950s, a lot of the Brotherhood's efforts were concentrated on getting the federal vote for Indians. As George used to say, "These politicians drive by the reserve, wave at us with one hand and thumb their noses with the other. They can tell us to go to hell because we can't do anything to bother them." In those days, the NAIB's preferred option was based on New Zealand's system, which guaranteed the Maori four seats in the national parliament. If we had our own seats in the House of Commons, our concerns would have to be heard. We might even hold the balance of power in a tightly divided House.

Self-government was another leading issue. All of us had seen the kinds of things Indian Agents did to control band councils. If we had the right to run our own communities under our own elected leaders, without being snookered or second-guessed by an appointed civil servant, we could wake the reserves up from the generations-long slumber that had left us so far behind the mainstream society.

And, if we were going to live our lives so much under the eye of the Government of Canada, then we ought at least to have our own department. Instead, we were under the Indian Affairs Branch of the Department of Citizenship and Immigration. That never made much sense to us, since under Canadian law we were not really citizens, and we certainly were not immigrants.

But the single overriding issue was land. All of us young Indians had grown up hearing the old-timers tell about how we were cheated out of our land. Not just about how the whites had moved in all over British Columbia, with neither treaty nor conquest, simply brushing us aside and setting up shop as if we didn't exist—but the dozens of instances, long after our reserve lands had been designated, when a nice piece of property would be "alienated" for the benefit of a white farmer or a prestigious golf course. Indian Agents, working hand in glove with political and business elites, often contrived to rob us of lands that should have been the basis of our livelihood and our identity. The Agents were paid to be watchdogs protecting us; instead some of them ran with the wolves.

In our parents' and grandparents' times, some of us had tried to get justice. The response from government: they made it illegal for Indians to engage legal counsel, or even to raise funds to hire a lawyer, to sue for return of the stolen lands. It was no wonder that, when my generation came up to bat, we saw political power as the only sure course for gaining redress of the wrongs that had been done to us.

We had some good allies, too. The legal adviser to the NAIB was Henry Castillou, son of the late judge Henry Castillou Sr. of the Cariboo. He was one of the few lawyers in those days who had a grasp of Indian legal issues in BC. He and his mother were prominent members of the Liberal Party's constituency association in the riding of Vancouver Centre—always the most important federal riding in BC, and almost always represented by a member of the federal Cabinet. In the late fifties, the Member of Parliament for the riding was J.R. Nicholson, who was later to become the Minister of Citizenship and Immigration.

I didn't know it as 1958 became 1959, but these people that I was meeting through George Manuel were soon to change my career, permanently and forever. But before that happened, I was to meet another person who was to have a profound impact on the rest of my life.

Donna Parr had recently come out from Ontario with a girlfriend, Barbara Shea. They were both young, both recently graduated as registered nurses, and both interested in seeing a different part of the country. They ended up in Kamloops as public health nurses, making the rounds of small communities as far up as Blue River, travelling by bus and train, looking after newborns and people who were nearing the other end of a lifespan.

They took an apartment on Columbia Street in Kamloops, next door to the home of a friend of mine, Sandy McCurrach, a fellow agriculture alumnus who had come to work in a feedstore that his father owned a portion of. Donna's idea of recreation was playing basketball in a women's league, which meant she was frequently seen coming in and going out wearing athletic shorts that showed her shapely legs to good advantage.

It wasn't long before I noticed that there was a very special person attached to those legs. We began dating in late 1959, and seven months later, in July 1960, we were married in her home town of North Bay. It was what they then called a mixed marriage—I was Catholic, Donna was United Church—and one of us had to give. I am sad to say that it hurt my mother when I left the church, but I had begun to drift away well before it came time to make a commitment to my wife. We did talk about maybe having a second ceremony sometime, in a Catholic church, but somehow it never happened.

Donna and I on our wedding day, July 16, 1960 in North Bay, Ontario

I have not been a church goer since the day we were married.

The Kamloops research station received permission to create a new research position; I applied for the job and was accepted. I can truthfully say that in the fall of 1960 I was happier than I had ever been before. I was back home. I had a beautiful wife. I was what I had long wanted to be and felt I was born to be: a scientist conducting research in range management, working in the field and the lab, finding it more fascinating than ever. I was now very glad I hadn't been offered the assistant superintendent's job at the Indian Agency.

I soon realized that a bachelor's degree was just the starting line if I wanted to make a career in agricultural research. So in the fall of 1961, I applied for educational leave and enrolled in a master's program at the University of Idaho, where I could study under Ed Tisdale, a Canadian who had earned a solid reputation in my area of interest. Much of his early work had been done at the Kamloops station, so he

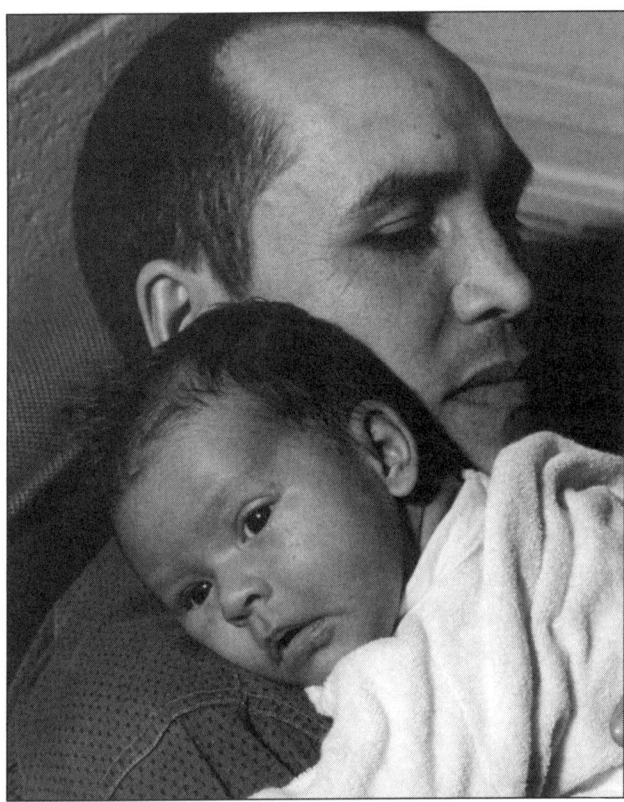

At grad school in Moscow, Idaho, with Lori Anne, our first born, January 1962

was the perfect advisor for my master's thesis, which I had determined would be an ecological study of sagebrush in BC.

Donna and I moved to Moscow, Idaho, where she got a job in the local hospital, and I took post-graduate classes—this time, they were paid for out of my own pocket; I'd had enough of going to Indian Affairs for a hand-out. But when I showed good marks in my first semester, the Department of Agriculture put me on half-pay while I completed the next two sessions. I then went back to Kamloops to complete my research and write my thesis. I defended it—that's academic jargon for presenting a scientific argument and answering questions about it from a panel of experts—and was awarded an A grade and my masters degree in forestry in the spring of 1964. Based on the research, I also co-authored a couple of scientific papers with my boss at the Kamloops Station, Dr. Alastair McLean.

I was on my way to a lifelong career in science, with a sideline in

social activism. Donna and I had brought two beautiful children into
the world, Lori Anne and Leonard Jr., and I was a reasonably respected member of the community. My next step was to have been a PhD;
I was talking to Professor Chuck Poulton of Oregon State University
and figuring out how to arrange more educational leave. The idea of
someday becoming a professor myself was highly appealing. I knew I
would be happy in the academic world.

But I was also still active with the North American Indian
Brotherhood, making speeches to Rotary Clubs and Chambers of
Commerce in the Cariboo and the Okanagan, and talking strategy
with George Manuel and his friends from the Vancouver Centre
Liberal Association.

We had won the vote in 1960. We were almost real persons under
Canadian law. Prime Minister John Diefenbaker had appointed James
Gladstone to be Canada's first Indian Senator in 1958 and that was a
great step forward. But George Manuel and Henry Castillou kept
reminding us that senators, though they can argue and lobby in the
caucus, don't often get their hands on the machinery of policy making. The real work takes place within individual government departments. For our people, the Indian Affairs Branch of the Department
of Citizenship and Immigration was where it was at and the key place
to be was in the Minister's office.

"What we need," George Manuel used to say, "is an Indian assistant to the Minister in Ottawa, somebody who sits at the table where
the decisions are made, somebody to speak for us." And then he
would look at me.

Through his Vancouver Centre contacts, he was talking up the
idea to Rene Tremblay, who was then the Minister. By the fall of 1964,
there was definite interest in Ottawa, and Raymond Denis, Tremblay's
executive assistant, was doing something that was unheard of: he was
coming out to attend meetings of the NAIB. The notion of an Indian
assistant to the Minister was gaining credibility, and—because of my
education—the NAIB leadership was looking to me as the candidate
for the job.

Then the whole thing fell apart: Raymond Denis did something
inappropriate involving an immigration case; it was not a good time

for Rene Tremblay to be making any unusual appointments to his staff. I went on being a contented research scientist in Kamloops until April of 1965. There was a cabinet shuffle in Ottawa, and the man who emerged as the new Minister of Citizenship and Immigration was none other than J.R. Nicholson, the MP for Vancouver Centre. I got a call from his executive assistant, Ross Fitzpatrick. Could I come to Vancouver to meet with the Minister?

I took the overnight sleeper train down to the city. We met at the Hotel Vancouver and talked for an hour or so. He offered me a job as his assistant, and I said, "I'll take it." I was willing to put my plans for a PhD on hold and go to Ottawa for a couple of years; I figured it would be an interesting experience and maybe I would make some good contacts that would be useful in my academic career. I didn't see it as a long-term commitment; I didn't know much about government, but even I knew that being a minister's assistant was a temporary job.

I thought J.R. Nicholson was a Minister who meant to make some changes. In 1965, he introduced a bill—which unfortunately died on the order paper when the House of Commons was dissolved for a general election—that would have created an Indian land claims commission. George Manuel and the NAIB activists felt that now was a time when real change could happen.

I also felt that I was personally obligated to accept the responsibility that went with the opportunity. It was the first time such a post had been offered to an Indian. I hoped I could do a lot to open doors for my people, and maybe help the bureaucrats in Indian Affairs to understand what it was like to be at the bottom of the pyramid they had built. I had long wanted to do something to help my people; now was the time to step forward and do what I could.

In late April, 1965, I left my office at the Kamloops Research Station. Donna and the kids and I caught the SuperContinental to Ottawa.

CHAPTER 2

"You should have a bullet..."

I n many ways, Canada is a much better country today than it was in that spring of 1965, but one thing I wish we could have kept from those times is the affordable transcontinental passenger train. There is just no better way to see Canada than through a train window, with the wheels clicking away the miles beneath you, while the land unrolls itself before your eyes. I knew the Cariboo and the Okanagan, and I had been up to Prince George and down to Vancouver and even over the mountains to Idaho, but now for the first time I was encountering the immense size and the great diversity of landscape that stretches east from the Rockies.

Donna and I held the kids on our laps and saw the dry grasslands of southern Alberta, with sometimes the far off specks that were pronghorn antelope, then the windblown wheatlands in Saskatchewan, with the clouds piled up on the edge of the world as if they had been swept there. I remember thinking that when I was finished whatever I was going to do in Ottawa, this would be a fascinating place for research into grassland ecology. Then it was on through Manitoba and suddenly into the woods, the pines and spruce so small compared to the big trees on the coast, but carpeting the rolling land as far as we could see; next came Superior's bare rocky shores, the grey lake itself as big as an ocean; finally, down through the farmlands into the Ottawa Valley, with tidy little towns that could have been copied from the picture on a jigsaw puzzle box, and into the old CPR station downtown, still then a working monument to the recently ended age of steam, not yet gutted and rejigged as a national conference centre.

It was a different Ottawa, three decades ago. No grand glass sky-scrapers had crept up to the base of Parliament Hill. It was an old fashioned, mid-sized Ontario city, built mostly of stone and red brick, although all of the Victorian-era legacies, like the Museum of Man and the neo-gothic Parliament Buildings themselves, were crusted by a century of deposited soot—the age of steam had also been the age of coal.

It was Ontario before the end of the blue laws: you couldn't see a movie or buy a tank of gas on a Sunday; weekdays, they rolled up the sidewalks come early evening. But for Donna and me, after Kamloops, this was the big city. And for an Indian, it was pretty well the centre of the universe.

For most non-aboriginals—and many of today's young Indians and Inuit—the word *Ottawa* is just shorthand for the whole panoply of their federal government. And for most Canadians, except during elections or times of major crisis, such as a Québec referendum, the doings of the national government are probably less important than what's going on at their jobs, or in their social lives, or in the National Hockey League. But for a thirty-one-year-old Indian in 1965, Ottawa was the alpha and omega. My whole life long, Ottawa had been the place where everything began and ended. It was a policy made in Ottawa that determined whether or not I could go to a public school, get a university education, cast a ballot. Ottawa set the structure of our lives in place around us, down to the smallest detail.

And now here I was, getting off the train, and preparing to start work in the office of the Minister who ran that structure. From now on, when my family on the reserve and my friends at the NAIB said, "if Ottawa decides this" or "if Ottawa agrees to that," I wouldn't be back there with them, thinking of a remote and distant source of power. I'd be where those decisions got made, maybe helping to shape them. After a lifetime of talking about Ottawa, I would *be* Ottawa.

We had made no arrangements in advance and spent a couple of weeks in a small hotel until we could find a place to rent. Being able to handle two rambunctious toddlers in such a small space was a trib-ute to Donna's mothering skills. By the time our household goods arrived by train, we had rented a small townhouse in Bayshore, then a distant suburb to the west of Ottawa.

In preparation for starting work, I took my only decent suit to the cleaners, who promptly lost it. Fortunately, the owner of the shop admitted fault and gave me money to buy a new one—the costs of moving and staying in a hotel had left us pretty broke—and there were no comfortable moving expense allowances for minister's assistants in those days. I managed to find a place on Rideau Street that was going out of business, and bought a three-button, charcoal-brown suit at half-price, in time to appear at the office on the day I was expected to start work.

It seems comical now, looking back on the picture of myself running downtown and frantically trying on pants and jackets. But it was a grimly serious business back then. To have arrived for work dressed poorly or to have come in a day late would have constituted a failure on my part to measure up. And I couldn't allow myself to fail.

Anytime I failed, it wouldn't just be me—it would be all of us failing, all of my kind. I could hear the voices in my head: *Well, what do you expect? Just another Indian who can't cut it.* I was breaking trail, being the first to do what I was doing, and I knew that—though it wasn't fair—we would all be judged by my performance. I would rather have had my legs broken than to have come in to work looking shabby or to have given the departmental officials a chance to say that the minister's new assistant was operating "on Indian time."

I found out later that the department was intensely curious about me, and that not everyone welcomed the idea of an Indian assistant to the Minister. They had pulled my file—all Indians had files that could be pulled—and kept the telephone lines warm between Ottawa and the district offices in Kamloops and Vernon. Some of the officials were supportive, but others reacted the way the doctors on a hospital policy committee would greet the prospect of a patient showing up at their monthly meeting and wanting to help make a few decisions. To use an Amos and Andy expression, those officials saw themselves as the work*ers*, and Indians as their work*ees*, and they didn't see any reason to confuse the roles.

But the bureaucrats weren't the only ones checking me out.

Within a few weeks of starting work, I had an unexpected visit from an Indian family who hailed from Wikwemikong on Manitoulin Island. There were four of them, Wilfred Pelletier, his sisters Yvonne and Rosemary, and his brother Tom. They dropped in one day and engaged me in a lengthy conversation about my background and opinions. Later, I found out that they were all strong supporters of the Prime Minister, Lester B. Pearson, whose riding included their reserve. They said they just came down to check me out.

Cabinet Ministers always have two offices, one on Parliament Hill and the other at their department's headquarters. The Hill office is mainly used for parliamentary business—meeting colleagues and delegations—while the departmental office is where the bulk of the policy and administrative work gets done. I was attached to Jack Nicholson's office at the Department of Citizenship and Immigration HQ at King Edward and Rideau in Ottawa's Lower Town.

These days, Ottawa's civil servants are accustomed to modern, climate-controlled office buildings with carpeted hallways, coordinated colour schemes and indirect lighting—virtually all of which have come about since my days as a minister's assistant. In the mid-1960s, much of the civil service worked in "temporary" structures that had been erected to handle the torrent of military and civilian personnel who had flooded into Ottawa to plan and conduct Canada's effort in World War II. The original shiny institutional paint, cracked linoleum and bare bulbs with green metal shades were still in place, a generation later. Jack Nicholson's departmental offices were in an extra storey that had been added on to the top of the Bourque Building. Unfortunately, the addition was none too securely attached to the original edifice: gusts of wind and the air conditioning unit on the roof gave the top floor a tendency to sway and vibrate. These conditions added an extra meaning to the term "green" as it applied to new staff. It was a couple of weeks before I got my sea legs and could get through a working day without a touch of motion sickness.

The job made me the conduit for everything going to or from the Minister that related to the Indian Affairs Branch of the department. Since I'd be seeing top-level documents, I needed a high-level security clearance, which involves information-gathering visits to family, friends and neighbours by the RCMP. As Donna and I came home one evening, not long after I started work, our neighbour Lise Hewlett met us in the townhouse hallway, very excited about an encounter with the Mounties' security service. "They were asking a lot of questions," she told us. "At one point, one of them asked us if it was true that you were a member of the Okanagan Band. I said I didn't even know that you played music."

As things worked out, I was with Jack Nicholson's office for only a few months. He was very much the image of a cabinet minister, always impeccably dressed and formal in his manners. Pierre Trudeau had yet to revolutionize the style of Canadian politics, and the media hadn't begun turning politicians into "just-plain-folks" celebrities. Nicholson took being a minister of the Crown very seriously, and made that plain the first time that we met. But he was also a kind man, and he treated me very well.

The office was run, to an ultra-efficient standard, by the Minister's

Chief Bob Smallboy of the Ermineskin Band, Hobbema, Alta. who came to Ottawa to visit the new Minister of Indian Affairs, Hon. J.R. (Jack) Nicholson, and reassert his people's treaty rights . Summer 1965

executive assistant, D. Ross Fitzpatrick, who would one day replace me as a Senator from British Columbia. Maybe it had all started with John F. Kennedy's 1961 inaugural address, when he told young Americans, "ask not what your country can do for you; ask what you can do for your country," but the sixties were a time when "the best and the brightest" did not let the low wages of public service deter them from putting their idealism into practice. D. Ross, as everyone called him, was one of those clever young men who had elected to serve his country for a while, when he could have been out making a fortune—a potential that he later demonstrated by developing a successful gold mine in California, then moving on to start a highly regarded vineyard outside Kelowna.

One thing I was thankful for was that neither D. Ross nor Jack Nicholson saw me as a token addition to the staff—an "Uncle Tomahawk" was one of the expressions of the time—but as just another working assistant. I don't know what I would have done if, after all the expectations of the people who had lobbied to get me to Ottawa, I had just turned out to be glorified window-dressing. I wanted to do the job and I knew I could do it: I'd earned a master's degree, and I'd published a few academic papers. But I never forgot that I had come from that little shoebox of a house at Six Mile Creek, and underneath all of my self-confidence, I think I was always listening for that voice that would stop me cold by saying, "Hey, Indian, what are you doing here?"

When the voice came, however, it wasn't a white man who was trying to pull me up short. It was a young Indian boy, part of a delegation led by Alma Greene of the Longhouse Group of the Six Nations that had come to make a presentation to the Minister. The Longhouse Group represented the more traditional segment of Iroquois society. Their ideas on how their society should be run were rooted in the pre-contact laws and customs of the Six Nations, which had been good enough to influence Benjamin Franklin's thinking on how Britain's American colonies should form a federation, and to provide models for Thomas Jefferson when he was drafting the US Constitution. Over these traditional ways, the Indian Act had laid an entirely different administrative and political structure, creating two different factions within the society: the Longhouse Group and what was called the "Indian Act" Group. They were often at loggerheads with each other.

Ordinarily, the Indian Affairs Branch did not deal directly with the Longhouse Group, but with their rivals. But I thought that since they were coming as a formal delegation, we should do them the honour of receiving them in some style, so I booked the Railway Committee Room in the Centre Block. It's the biggest room on Parliament Hill, hung with chandeliers and decorated with large paintings depicting Canadian transportation themes, and it's where many state functions and important ceremonies are held. The room was set up in committee hearing style, with a table for the Minister and his officials (including me) and rows of chairs for the twenty-five or so members of the Longhouse Group.

The Iroquois culture was a matriarchy, and Alma Greene was a strong woman of great dignity. She took the Minister and us officials on a journey through Six Nations history leading up to the present conflict. I had already researched the issues and personalities, like a good assistant, and had briefed the Minister in advance. We knew that the Longhouse Group hadn't come to give the Minister an honourary membership, but the exchanges were polite, and I thought it had at least been a useful exercise in educating all of us in some of the complexities Ottawa had created by slapping a we-know-what's-best, one-size-fits-all administrative blanket over the dozens of diverse and intricate social structures that had been evolving through uncounted centuries before the whites arrived.

When the presentations were over at about nine in the evening, we all adjourned to some buffet tables on the other side of the room, where the Parliamentary restaurant had provided coffee and juice and trays of hors d'oeuvres. The Minister, his officials and the Longhouse Group were engaged in the kind of small talk and informal face-to-face contact that can often be a more important part of a political relationship than the formal speeches and position papers. I was circulating through the crowd when I saw one of the youngest members of the delegation, a clean-cut boy in his mid-teens, making his way toward me.

I was feeling good about how well the event had gone, everyone so polite and dignified, and I was sure the Minister had learned something. I thought this young fellow with the serious expression might be coming to ask me about my work—*"Gee, how can I get to be a minister's assistant when I grow up?*—so it set me back on my heels when he put his face up close to mine and hissed, "You should be ashamed of yourself! Call yourself an Indian, sitting up there next to that white man Minister! You should have a bullet, right here!" And he put his finger to the middle of his forehead.

It took me a moment to recover, but then I told him what I thought I was doing in Ottawa, trying to make a difference from the inside where the power was, where the decisions got made. It was the first installment of a continuing conversation with radical—and sometimes not-so-radical—Indians that I would have time and again over the ensuing three decades. As far as I know, I never changed any of their minds, including that teenager. They went on calling me a sell-out, a brown-skinned white man, an "apple" who was red on the outside and white on the inside.

It hurt because often I found myself on the side of the power when it was the people—my people—who were on the right side of the issues. It felt like hell, and I would ask myself, "Am I doing the right thing? Am I doing any good?" I remember the Indian journalist Doug Cuthand asking me, "What the hell are you doing with those Liberals? You should be fighting for us in the opposition."

It would have been a lot easier to be a critic, I know that. It's always easier to wear your heart on your sleeve and to stand on the sidelines preaching and shouting slogans. You can go home feeling that you're pure of heart and firmly on the side of the angels. But you get up the next day and nothing has changed. Sure, you've got off guilt-free, never having had to compromise or bite your tongue when you wanted to spit out whatever was turning over in your belly. But you're the only one who benefits from your self-indulgence. Nobody gets a better house. Nobody gets a loan to buy a fish boat or build a farm. Nobody gets a job or an education. So I stuffed my doubts where they wouldn't get in the way and went on doing my job in Jack Nicholson's office, though I never forgot that Iroquois boy's bullet.

Indians generally despised the Indian Affairs Branch. I hated the system it had imposed upon us. But many—maybe even most—of the people who worked in that system were well-intentioned, decent human beings. The head man in the bureaucracy was R.F. (Bob) Battle, the Assistant Deputy Minister for the Indian Affairs Branch, who reported to Claude Isbister, the Deputy Minister for the whole Citizenship and Immigration Department. As the Minister's liaison with the IAB, I got to know Bob Battle well enough that once our initial mutual suspicions were overcome, he would tell me about the bitter frustration he sometimes felt in trying to make the system deliver for the people who were struggling along beneath it. The anxiety was literally eating away at him: he had developed an ulcer.

The IAB was full of well-meaning men like him and like Eric Underwood, the assistant superintendent at the Vernon office who had lent me a typewriter to take to university. They went to work every day and did their jobs, but the process that they administered just didn't function. We found that out in spades when we mounted a national tour by the Minister to inspect Indian housing on the reserves.

The state of housing on reserves in the mid sixties was nothing short of a national disgrace. Since the end of the Second World War, the rest of rural Canada had been coming into the twentieth century, with electrification and piped-in water. But that progress had mainly been due to the growing activism of provincial and municipal governments. Indian reserves, under federal jurisdiction, were still stuck in the nineteenth century: heated by wood stoves, lit by oil lamps, watered by buckets hauled from lakes and streams, and each with the inevitable outhouse.

The glaring contrast between reserves and other rural areas had been highlighted at a federal provincial conference on poverty and opportunity held in Ottawa in 1965. The *Globe and Mail* ran a number of strongly worded articles on conditions on Alberta reserves, and other newspapers took up the cause. The statistics told the story: only nine per cent of homes on reserves were connected to sewers or septic tanks; only 13 per cent had running water; only seven per cent had a bathtub. The IAB, led by George Bowen, the head of the housing department, was urging Nicholson to conduct a national tour, and I added my voice during a meeting with the Minister: "We have to go and see it, first-hand, and take along people from outside the department who can make something happen."

After the House of Commons rose for the summer, we began the first leg of the tour with a visit to the Fort William Indian Band in July. The town of Fort William had amalgamated with Port Arthur to form Thunder Bay in 1964, but the reserve still bore the same old name—perhaps there was some symbolism in that. Chief Frank Pelletier awarded Jack Nicholson an honourary chieftainship, which pleased the Minister quite a bit. Along with the title, they also gave him an Ojibway name, but I can't remember what it was. That was the only part of the tour that was pleasant to remember; from there on in, it got pretty grim.

We had assembled a high-powered group. Besides the Minister, Bob Battle and George Bowen, we were accompanied by Tom Kent, principal secretary to Prime Minister Pearson, and Herb Higgnet, President of Central Mortgage and Housing Corporation, as it was then known. We had a government plane, and from Thunder Bay we gradually worked our way west over the next ten days, flying in to the airport nearest to a targeted reserve, to be met by local officials in departmental cars and then driven down dusty roads into sheer heartbreak.

I had been raised on a small, rural reserve, and I thought I had a pretty good idea of what poverty looked like. But the things I saw on that trip shook me. I saw three or four families, fifteen or twenty people, crammed into the few rooms of mouldering log cabins. I saw houses—shacks, would be a better word—with broken doors, with plastic sheets in place of window panes, with shingles blown off or rotted away. I walked through villages that had never seen a light bulb or a water tap, where the garbage piled up between the houses because there were no trucks to haul it away.

I will never forget one little place in the Northwest Territories, somewhere south of Great Slave Lake. A very old man, an elder, was living in a tiny log cabin, about six feet wide and not much more than that in length. Inside were a small wood stove and a table of rough boards and his bed—there was no room for anything else. He said he preferred it small, because then it was easier to heat. I remember thinking, "My God, this man sleeps in a dump not much bigger than a doghouse, and he is trying to spare all of us the embarrassment of his poverty."

I had to walk away for a few minutes. I didn't want anyone to see that there were tears in my eyes. Besides, I thought I might actually throw up the tasty and nourishing breakfast we had eaten before coming out to this place of destitution. The Minister was equally affected. It's one thing to sit in a committee room and be told about poverty; it's another thing entirely to stand in the midst of its sights and smells. Jack Nicholson's face was pale, and there was a crack in his voice as he said, "How do we help these people?"

By the time we were standing outside the band hall on the Kamloops reserve, the last night on the trip, the Minister and the officials were still asking that same question. And I was giving them the same answer I always gave: the ultimate solution was for my people to get educated, so we could get jobs and build our own businesses, out from under that big smothering blanket that Ottawa laid over every reserve, every status Indian who lived inside the system. We had to be able to make our own choices and be responsible for our own lives.

One big step toward that kind of independence would be for Indians to have equal access to the government programs that had helped build a modern Canada since the end of the war. Indians had to be able to get a CMHC-guaranteed loan like anyone else. That meant changing the National Housing Act, which—like a lot of federal legislation in those days—specifically barred aboriginal people from receiving benefits. We stood there in the Kamloops night and decided that that was the way to go: we had to begin pulling down the walls that kept Indians separate and far from equal.

Did that mean we went right back to Ottawa and started drafting a bill? No, it didn't. I was learning that government doesn't often get where it's going by straight lines, moving smoothly from A to B and on to C. It's more like a zig here and a zag there, with a sudden detour over to put out some unexpected fire; sometimes everything stops for

a while until the batteries that store political will have built up
enough of a charge to make change possible. We didn't even complete
the eastern half of the national housing tour. Events intervened in the
form of a general election. So I suppose that fourteen-year-old
Iroquois boy might have said that our visit did no good for that old
man. We came, we saw, we went back to Ottawa, and he was still
where we had left him.

But the fact is, we did do some good, ultimately a lot of good,
although it took years to amend the National Housing Act so that it
included Indians. The legislation came in the fall of 1968, and was
accompanied by amendments to the Farm Credit Act and other
statutes as an economic development package. The key was to have
the government guarantee the loans that were made on reserves. Jean
Chrétien was the new Minister who introduced the bill, but the package was readied by Art Laing. By the time it was passed, it had taken
four years to turn the bureaucratic gears, produce the legislation and
get it through the Commons. That was one of the things that was
becoming clear to me in my first months as a minister's assistant—
that the wheels of Ottawa grind slowly, when they grind at all.

Certainly, the process of changing those laws was not as dramatic
as occupying an Indian Affairs office or blockading a road. But it put
roofs over thousands of Indian families and connected them to sewers and water pipes. To me, that is a serious accomplishment, and the
seeds of it were sown in the summer of 1965 when those white men
in suits went out to the remote reserves and came face to face with the
horrific consequences of the system they were responsible for.

In the meantime, the big question facing me as 1965 wound to a
close, was whether I would still have a job in Ottawa or whether it was
time to go back to the academic world and start working on my PhD.
In September, Lester Pearson called on Governor General Georges
Vanier to dissolve the House, and we went into a general election. I
did not play any role in the campaign; although I had been a member of the Liberal Party for five years and had worked on a minister's
staff for several months, I didn't think of myself as a political animal.
I was there to try to influence government policy on behalf of my people, which made me a little more than a spectator but not actually a

player. So while the election rolled on, and the Minister and D. Ross went back to Vancouver to fight it, I stayed in the office and answered inquiries—mostly from opposition MPs—as best I could.

It was a fascinating time to be watching Canadian politics from the box seats. The main parties were led by three of the most out-standing men our history has produced—Lester Pearson, John Diefenbaker and Tommy Douglas—but there was a feeling that some-how we were seeing the last act of their story and that something new would soon be coming in from the wings. Much of the coverage dur-ing the election centred on three star candidates from Québec known as the "Three Wise Men"—Gerard Pelletier, Jean Marchand and Pierre Trudeau—who were all expected to make their way to the front benches.

When the votes were counted on November 8, Pearson once again came up a few seats short of a majority. When he put together his new cabinet, he shuffled Jack Nicholson over to the labour portfolio and put Art Laing, the MP for Vancouver South, in charge of Indian Affairs. I didn't expect Nicholson to take me with him to Labour where I would have been of no particular use; I did hope for a call from Art Laing's executive assistant, Gordon Gibson, who until recently wrote for the *Globe and Mail*, but as the days lengthened into weeks, the phone did not ring.

Nothing was ever said, but I got the impression that Laing felt I might have had only token status in Nicholson's office; if so, he had no use for me. Once again, it appeared that I was being quietly checked out behind the scenes. It probably helped that the new Minister hailed from Vancouver, where my old NAIB mentor Henry Castillou would have been staunchly standing up for me. Finally just before Christmas, Gibson called and asked me to come in for a chat, and I went back to work in January 1966.

But not to Citizenship and Immigration. The Prime Minister had acquiesced to what the NAIB and many other voices had long been calling for, and had created a separate ministry for Indian affairs. There was some quiet to-ing and fro-ing behind closed doors over the name of the new department. Originally, it was to have been called the Department of Indian and Northern Affairs, but the word

"Development" had been made part of the department's title at the insistence of its first Minister, the former Minister of Northern Affairs, Art Laing. I heard that he had told the Prime Minister that he wouldn't take the job unless it was clear that this was to be an activist department, and he wanted that reflected in the name.

Laing was in many ways a contrast to Jack Nicholson. I couldn't easily picture him in top hat and tails. He was short and stocky with a thick neck and a tendency to stick out his chin at any challenge. I liked that he had won a degree in Agriculture from UBC in the twenties. And I liked his attitude toward my people, as reflected in his insistence on making development the cornerstone of his approach to Indian Affairs. He summed up that attitude in a brief speech I heard him make to a group of Saskatchewan Indians in early 1966. He said, "I'm going to do my best for you, but every Minister of Indian Affairs before me has been a failure, and I will be a failure, too. Things will be right for you only when you have complete control over your individual lives, and you make all your own decisions."

One of the reasons why every Indian Affairs minister had been a failure cropped up not long after Laing took on the job. We found out that the system had a dynamic and a direction all its own, whatever the political leadership might want. It happened after the Minister and I toured a Huron reserve in Québec. The place was highly organized—the people were manufacturing lacrosse sticks, moccasins and canoes—and everyone was making a good living out of their enterprises. The Band's Chief, Max Gros-Louis, proudly told us, "Nobody's on welfare on my reserve."

But the Hurons were constrained by their reserve's small size. They needed more land, and Chief Gros-Louis wanted to enlist the Minister's aid in a proposal to buy 125 nearby acres that were on the market. The system being what it was, no Indian band could make that kind of decision; only the Great White Father in Ottawa had the power to say yes or no. Or so we thought.

Art Laing was gung-ho to help the Hurons. "I'm impressed as hell by these people," he said to me. "We're going to help them buy that land." But when he told his officials what we had in mind, he came up against a roadblock. Bob Battle, by now an Assistant Deputy

Minister of the new department, was clearly taken aback. "Minister," he said, "it's our policy that there will be no additions to Indian reserves. No more land for Indians."

I was surprised. I'd been an Indian all my life and an activist for many years, and that was the first I'd heard of the "no new land" policy. It was obviously news to Art Laing, too. I can remember him pausing and looking around at Battle and the other officials seated in a circle in his office. "Whose policy is that?" he asked, quietly.

"The department's," was the answer.

"The department does not make policy," Laing said, just as quietly. "The Minister does. And I am the Minister. My policy is to help those people to help themselves."

What followed was a gentlemanly struggle. The department marshalled its arguments and precedents and presented them to the Minister over the next couple of weeks in both written and oral form. It was an impressive case, and well reasoned, but it started from the time honoured bureaucratic premise that nothing should ever be done for the first time. Laing's position was that the system should serve the people; if it didn't, then the system had to change.

The Hurons got to buy the land. I worked on the project over the next few months, and Chief Max Gros-Louis and I grew to be good friends. He was one of a number of the older generation of Indian leaders whom I came to know during my days as an assistant: James Gosnell, Simon Baker and Guy Williams from BC; Howard Beebe, Bob Smallboy and Jim Shot Both Sides of Alberta; John Tootoosis and Walter Dieter in Saskatchewan; Jean Cuthand and Dave Courschene from Manitoba; Omer Peters and Wilmer Nadjiwon in Ontario; Andrew Delisle and Mary Two-Axe Early from Québec; and Wallace LaBillois from the Atlantic.

There were also a few Indians who had found careers in the department's head office. Les Smith was a senior official in the housing department; he was the brother of Harry Smith, the Brantford-born Mohawk who was better known by his stage name, Jay Silverheels, and famous the world over as the Lone Ranger's sidekick, Tonto. Gordon Miller was a generalist who worked in the membership section—the question of whether an individual was or wasn't a

With Les Smith, a Mohawk from Six Nations, Ontario, editor of "The Indian News". in 1965. Les was the brother of Harry Smith A.K.A. Jay Silverheels A.K.A. "Tonto"

status Indian was often the department's first concern. And I worked often with Gilbert (Slim) Monture, a geologist who had become a senior advisor to the department after a brilliant career in the old Department of Munitions and Supply under the legendary C.D. Howe.

Many of the old-line Indian leadership had been active in the National Indian Advisory Council (NIAC), a precursor to the National Indian Brotherhood (NIB). The NIAC played a useful role in trying to keep departmental policy in tune with the kinds of goals Indians were reaching for in the fifties and sixties. Its members formed a loosely connected network all across the country—sometimes referred to as the "moccasin telegraph"—and they were well respected in their own communities. If the department could have used them as more than a sounding board—that is, if they had been enlisted to help create policy instead of only being asked to react to it—their talents would have been better employed.

One of the most active members of the Advisory Council was Guy Williams, a Tsimshian from Kitimat. He was a highly intelligent man, and president of the Native Brotherhood, a BC organization founded by the Haida Alfred Adams in 1931. In 1966, Guy Williams and I began working on a project to help West Coast Indian fishermen free themselves from a system that verged on debt slavery to the fish packing companies. BC's coastal Indians had been fishing those waters since the end of the last ice age, and they were (and still are) a fiercely independent crowd. They were as productive and competitive as anyone, but they were handicapped by the Indian Affairs system: Indians had no access to the capital needed to buy better boats and gear. Many of them ended up owing their souls to the packers.

I was able to arrange for Guy Williams to come to Ottawa and meet with the Deputy Minister of Fisheries, Dr. A.W. Needler—the first time that any Indian fisherman had been able to put a case to a national decision-maker. With Art Laing's enthusiastic backing, Fisheries Minister Hedard Robichaud put together a $500,000 Indian Fisheries Assistance Program, which in time came to be administered by the Native Brotherhood itself. That program helped a lot of Indian fishermen to maintain their independence and carry on with a way of life that had been theirs since time immemorial.

By the time that program was announced, the calendar had rolled around to 1967. I had spent two years in Ottawa and had become a competent minister's assistant. I liked the man I was working for, and I felt that the achievements we were making, though often small and incremental, were adding up to some genuinely positive changes for my people. I had established a network of contacts throughout DIAND, as well as in other departments like Agriculture and Fisheries. I wasn't on anybody's list of major movers and shakers, but I was making a contribution.

My big continuing project was helping Art Laing create a wide-ranging economic development package that would extend to Indians the benefits available to all other Canadians under federal programs like the National Housing Act. It had been almost two years since Jack Nicholson and I had started that national housing tour and come to the conclusion that Indians needed to have access to CMHC funds. It had also made sense to apply the principle of equal access to capital to other federal statutes, such as the Farm Credit Corporation and Small Business Loans Acts. As always, the Ottawa mills were

grinding ever slowly—but at least we were providing more grist for
the millstones—and the package, when it was eventually made law
under Jean Chrétien, would help a lot of native entrepreneurs and
farmers stand on their own feet.

Art Laing had come to trust my judgment enough for him to hand
me the responsibility for selecting the first Indian member of the
Territorial Council of the Northwest Territories. It offended my
Minister's strong sense of democracy that the NWT was still being run
by a Territorial Council dominated by unelected white southerners
operating in Ottawa. During the 1965 election campaign, the Prime
Minister had appointed Abraham Okpik, an Inuit journalist and
translator, to the Council. Now Laing had resolved to appoint the first
Indian member.

He called me into his office and told me he was sending me on a
tour of the north. I was to visit the main communities in the western
arctic, sound out the opinions of the people, and come back to him
with a candidate he could recommend to Lester Pearson. I flew out to
Yellowknife and began criss-crossing the barrens, touching down in
Inuvik, Fort McPherson, Fort Ray, Fort Simpson, Hay River and Fort
Smith. I met with chiefs and community leaders, local people from
the department, and with a lot of just plain folks, talking Indian to
Indian with the officials out of the way. Wherever I went, the same
name kept coming up. John Tetlitchi Charlie was a Gwitch'in Dene
chief, a hunter and trapper who had become the most respected
leader among his people. Once I had met him at Fort McPherson, I
had no hesitation in recommending him to Art Laing.

The Minister named him to the Territorial Council, and John
Tetlitchi Charlie's appointment—as Laing had anticipated—took the
governance of the north a step closer to what he and I believed it
should be: a matter that was nobody's business but that of the northern peoples themselves. In September, 1967, the Territorial Council
was moved to Yellowknife, where it belonged, and by 1974 all of its
members would be elected. Since the population of the NWT was
mainly Indian and Inuit, so were most of the people elected to the
Council. It was the first demonstration to Canadians that aboriginal
people could govern themselves. The democratic process that has

*With R.F.(Bob)
Battle, Deputy
Minister ,1966.*

now led to the creation of the new Territory of Nunavut is Art Laing's enduring legacy, achieved with a strong assist from Stuart Hodgson, the burly former labour union boss who was Laing's appointee as Commissioner, and who had pretty blunt views on any system that did not reflect the will of the people.

~~~~~

With the summer of 1967 came the Centennial and Expo, and all at once it was just a wonderful thing to be a Canadian. Something was happening to us as a country and as individuals. It was as if we'd all been in a cocoon, and now daylight was suddenly breaking in and inviting us to stretch our wings. The world was opening up in ways we'd never anticipated. We'd come a hundred years down the road, and there was a sense that we'd only just begun to know who we were.

If that was the effect of the Centennial year on Canadians in general, 1967 was a breakthrough year for my people. It was decided that Expo would have a pavilion honouring Canada's Indian peoples, and such was the strange and heady spirit of the time that responsibility for staging the exhibition was handed over to Indians. To the young Indians of today, that probably seems the obvious way to go, but in 1967 it was revolutionary—for generations, our people had been buried under a system that treated us like backwards children, and now we were being trusted to tell the world exactly who *we* thought we were.

The Department of Indian Affairs and Northern Development (DIAND) was heavily involved in the pavilion project, and I spent a lot of time helping to overcome the thousand and one obstacles that popped up in the planning and construction of the exhibit. But the credit belonged to the Indians who brought it all together: Chief Andrew Delisle of the Kahnewake Mohawks, who was appointed Commissioner of the pavilion; Russ Moses of the Six Nations, a Korean War vet and editor of *Indian News*, who handled the media and promotions; Joe Francis, the department's architect, who was given permission to brush aside managers who got in his way; Bernard Assiniwi, from the department's cultural affairs section, who chose the pavilion's front-line staff; and Duke Redbird, who wrote most of the hard-hitting text that told the story of what had happened to our peoples since we first welcomed the white man to our land.

If it had been left to the bureaucrats and academics—the "usual suspects" who showed up at university-sponsored conferences on the "native problem"—the Indians of Canada pavilion would probably have emerged as a cross between an anthropologist's display of "leathers-and-feathers" and some strange Disneyish production. But millions of white Canadians went in through the door of that concrete pavilion and came out with a whole new picture of what it meant to be an Indian in Canada. Their encounter with a beautifully rendered but soul-gripping reality probably did more to change the status of our people in the next thirty years than a thousand footnoted studies.

As part of the Centennial celebrations, Queen Elizabeth came to Expo and to Ottawa. Never having been much for monarchy—despite the special historical relationship that is supposed to have existed between Canadian Indians and the British Crown since the days of Victoria, "the Grandmother"—I didn't pay much attention to plans for the royal visit. That is, not until I received a phone call from Mary Macdonald, the Prime Minister's executive assistant, with whom I sometimes worked on issues involving Indian bands in Lester Pearson's northern Ontario riding.

She said, "Len, are you sitting down?"

I said I was, and she told me that I had been selected as one of fifty "outstanding young Canadians" who were invited to have dinner with the Queen at Rideau Hall, the Governor Generals' residence. Art Laing had put my name forward without telling me. I thought, "Wow, I'm going to need a tux." Then I called Donna, and said, "Are you sitting down?"

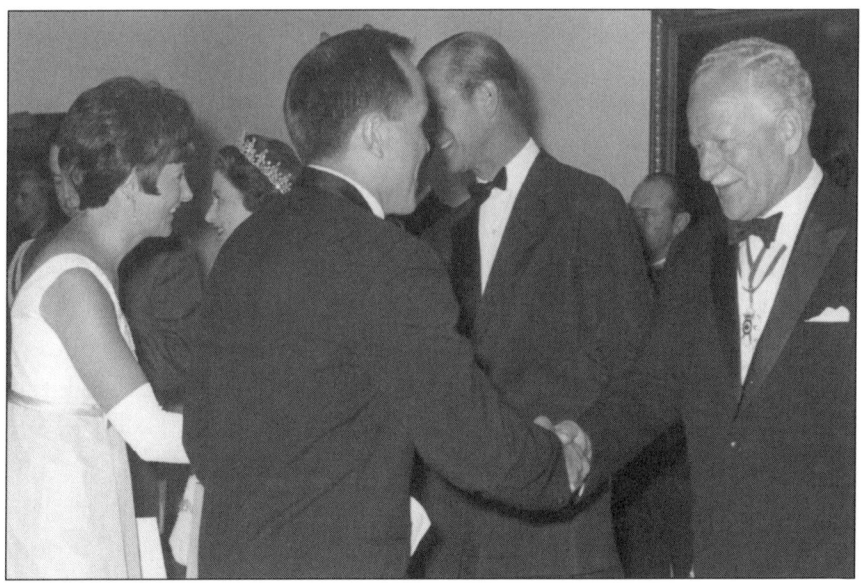

Donna and I meeting Queen Elizabeth, Prince Philip, and Governor General Roland Michener in the receiving line to attend the banquet for fifty outstanding young Canadians at Government House during Expo 1967.

We drove up to Rideau Hall in our two-year-old Chevy Biscayne—
the bare bones utility model. I dropped Donna off at the door and
parked around the side, directed by a Mountie in red serge. Then I
came around and escorted Donna into the foyer of Roland Michener's
official residence. It was like something out of a movie: crystal chandeliers, oil paintings of former Governors General on the walls, and a
very prominent picture of Her Majesty in her robes of state.

I thought we made a pretty interesting crowd, we fifty hand-
picked up-and-comers in our twenties and thirties. Patrick Watson of
the CBC's *This Hour Has Seven Days* was one of us. So was Olympic
skiing champion Nancy Greene and actress Genevieve Bujold. The
GG's footmen helped us form a receiving line, then the Queen,
dressed in a formal gown, came and shook hands with all of us.
Prince Philip stood beside her. I bowed and Donna curtsied. Nobody
had told us the rules—no touching, no speaking until you're spoken
to—but fortunately, I didn't inadvertently do anything foolish. We all
trooped in for dinner—which was superb—in a grand and glittering
room, and the Queen gave a brief speech and wished us well, and that
was all there was to it.

Talking about it with Donna as we drove home to our little townhouse in Bayshore, it seemed to me that there had been no real contact between any of us and the royals. Neither the Queen nor Philip
had cracked a smile or circulated around to talk to anyone. We might
as well have been an animated backdrop. I had the same impression,
some years later, when I was in the cabinet and she came to a state
dinner for Privy Councillors in Ottawa during the 1976 Olympics.

But I wasn't thinking about royalty as Donna and I drove home
from Rideau Hall that summer night in 1967. It felt as if our time in
Ottawa was coming to an end. The Conservatives appeared to be
about to dump the old Chief, John Diefenbaker, as head of their
party. Among the Liberals, everyone expected Lester B. to call it quits
in the next few months, once the smoke had cleared from the Tory
contest. There would be a leadership campaign in the spring; then we
would be into an election.

"I guess it's time to think about going home," I said to Donna. I'd
given the NAIB two years, but now I was pushing 34 years of age, and

I still had my PhD to earn. We agreed we'd stay until the election, then head on back to Kamloops. I was sure my old job as a research officer would be waiting for me at the Kamloops agricultural station. With all my good Ottawa contacts, I would be a handy guy to have around.

The Tory convention came and went in September. It was a brutal affair for Diefenbaker, and I felt sorry for him, watching him lose it all in the glare of the TV lights. Many Indians of my generation have a soft spot in our hearts for Diefenbaker; we remember that it was his government that finally gave us the vote.

With Bob Stanfield as the new head of the Conservatives, the Liberals began to stir in the back rooms. As we moved toward Christmas, there were phone calls and quiet conversations in which ministers and backbenchers felt each other out. Many of the young party activists who worked in ministers' offices were getting that sharp glint in the eye that is the precursor to the wide-eyed frenzy of a leadership campaign. On December 14, Lester Pearson opened the gates and let loose the hounds.

Looking back on it now, there's a tendency to reorganize events through hindsight: Pearson quit, Trudeaumania broke out, and Pierre Trudeau waltzed easily into office. But the fact was, except among the young assistants, Trudeau was by no means the first choice of many Liberal insiders. To much of the old guard, he seemed kind of flaky, and not on the same level as such well-established powers as Paul Martin, Mitchell Sharp and Robert Winters. As Justice Minister since April 1967, he had shepherded a liberalized divorce law through Parliament and had recently introduced an omnibus set of amendments to the Criminal Code that allowed abortions to be performed and legalized homosexual acts between consenting adults in private. On this last issue, Trudeau had caught the attention of press and public by declaring, "There is no place for the state in the bedrooms of the nation," but that didn't make him anybody's idea of a front runner to replace Lester Pearson.

For what it was worth, I liked him. I say, "for what it was worth," because my support was not being sought by any candidate. Although I was a party member, and had spent two-and-a-half years rubbing shoulders with a few of the bright lights for whom service in a minister's office was part of a political apprenticeship, I was not "one of the boys." I had remained an outsider among the insiders, a sojourner who would be heading home to resume an interrupted career. Art Laing's executive assistant, however, was definitely an insider: Gordon Gibson's father, Gordon Gibson Sr., was the legendary "Bull of the Woods" of BC politics, the Liberal Member of the Legislative Assembly who had almost single-handedly exposed corruption in the granting of provincial forest licences, which led to the arrest and conviction of Socred Forest Minister Bob Sommers—the first time in the history of the entire Commonwealth that a cabinet minister had gone to jail. The son lived and breathed politics, and he had one of the sharpest analytical minds I had encountered in Ottawa.

On one of those clear bright days that sometimes make February almost bearable in our nation's capital, while I was taking a walk down Kent Street after lunch, I ran into Gordon Gibson. "What do you think of Trudeau?" he asked me. It was the first time he had asked my opinion on a purely political matter. I said what a lot of young Canadians were thinking in those days: we needed new blood, somebody born in the 20th century, a leader who embodied that sense of *We're Canadians; we can do anything* that had come out of the Centennial year. It didn't hurt that Trudeau was a completely bilingual Québecer: the FLQ had been blowing up Montreal mailboxes and it was only a few months since Charles de Gaulle had shouted "Vive le Québec libre" from the balcony of the Montreal city hall. The country was becoming increasingly edgy about Québec.

"I'm going to go work on his campaign," Gordon said. A few days later, Trudeau announced his candidacy, and Gordon left Art Laing's office. For Laing himself, the leadership race was a torment; he could not decide where to put his support. He was impressed by Trudeau's intellect, but told me, "The guy just doesn't look like a prime minister." The sandals, longish hair and sports car were too much for the old UBC agriculture grad. There was a generational divide in the Liberal Party in the spring of 1968, and it ran between Art Laing and Gordon Gibson. Laing held out until the convention then finally went to Bob Winters.

I had met Trudeau a couple of times before he ran for the leadership. MPs and minister's assistants didn't mix much in those days—minister's staff were expected to be workaholics attached to their desks by invisible chains—but I had had the opportunity to talk with him when he hitched a ride on a Ministry of Transport Viscount airplane that Laing had booked to take us out to visit some Indian communities in the west. Trudeau was going canoeing somewhere in the Northwest Territories, and flew with us as far as Edmonton.

The interior of the Viscount was configured so that ministers and their staff and officials could work as they flew; there were comfortable chairs grouped in the middle of the plane. But Trudeau sat by himself in a less comfortable seat in the forward end of the cabin, reading a book on constitutional law. He had recently been made Minister of Justice, and most people knew very little about him.

I went up and introduced myself; he invited me to sit down, and we talked for a while. Some newspaper writers would later characterize Trudeau as a chilly, intellectual kind of guy, but to me he was warm and friendly. And genuine: most Indians who spend a lot of time with white folks develop a reliable instinct for knowing when we are being patronized or tolerated just for the sake of politeness—you see a certain look behind the eyes. I saw nothing like that in Pierre Trudeau. I also didn't see any charisma; he looked to me like the kind of guy you'd come across in the faculty lounge of any university.

In the years to come, we came to know each other a lot better. I was always known as a Trudeau loyalist, and for a very simple reason: he never failed to treat me well. And I was always convinced that he had a feeling for our people, that he wanted to do something for us. Even when he said that there was "no such thing as aboriginal rights," I recognized that he was being the law professor, just giving the legal position, and I wasn't offended by it. I just thought he was wrong.

I had nothing to do with the leadership campaign, though I cheered Trudeau from the sidelines. As the party turned inward, I held down the fort in Art Laing's office, along with northern affairs assistant David Ingram. But on April 6, I went to the convention as an observer, sitting high up in the rafters as the party powers clashed down there amid all the hoopla on the floor. It was the most exciting public event I had ever been to, and as the balloting continued, I was literally biting my nails.

Over the next sixteen years, Trudeau would come to dominate the party so completely that many would forget that it was a narrow margin that had made him leader and Prime Minister. Not all the faces were smiling as we went out into the spring night. But I was overjoyed. Something new was going to happen. We had a Prime Minister who really gave a damn about Indians.

And as for me, I'd be heading home.

The election was expected early. Trudeau moved up the date for being sworn in as Prime Minister because delaying his investiture might have meant waiting till the fall to go to the people. That suited me. I had told Art Laing I was leaving and was making arrangements to get my old job back. Then I came home to find a telegram waiting for me. Sandy McCurrach, my old classmate who worked in his father's feedstore in Kamloops, wired to say that he had been talking to a few people around town, and everybody wanted me to go for the Liberal nomination.

The incumbent MP for Kamloops in those days was E. Davie Fulton, the senior Tory in British Columbia and former Minister of Justice in the Diefenbaker government, who had been a major contender for the recently decided Conservative leadership. I didn't see me making much of a dent in Davie Fulton. He amounted to a pretty respectable Goliath for this little Indian David.

I read Sandy's telegram twice, and both times, I looked at Donna and said, "Run against Davie Fulton? Who, me?"

CHAPTER 3

A willing horse

T he summer I was seventeen, a Chinese gardener named Johnny Quong hired my father to clear the weeds from his tomato fields. He did this every year, using a horse-drawn cultivator, which is a farming implement with several small blades like miniature ploughshares that can be set at different heights. The horse pulled the cultivator up and down between the rows of tomato plants, uprooting the weeds that would otherwise choke out the crop.

It was a tricky business, calling for a knowledgeable horse at one end and an experienced handler at the other. If things got out of control, a lot of valuable tomato plants could end up ruined. Normally, my father would take Shorty, our dependable black work horse, and do the job himself. But, this summer, he said I would come with him. I would have the black, and he would use King, a bawley bay who didn't know as much as Shorty, but would be all right with my dad's hands on the reins. With two horses and two men, we would get two dollars an hour instead of one, and that meant a lot to the family budget.

Farming requires a different set of skills than moving cattle around. I had never done this kind of work before, and I was pretty petrified. When we had led the horses down to the field in the summer heat and hitched them to the cultivators, I told my dad I was really nervous about making a mistake.

Maybe a modern father would put his arm around an anxious teenager and say something reassuring. My father looked at me, his face stern, and said a few words in Okanagan that roughly translate as, "Don't make a fool of yourself." But as anyone who is fluent in two languages can tell you, much is often lost in translation. In Okanagan, that simple phrase hauls a lot of freight behind it. A fuller translation might be something like this: "Don't act in a way that will cause you to lose your dignity."

But that still wouldn't get the real message across. It wouldn't convey how important dignity is to our people. If I screwed up in that tomato field, with the Chinese farmers looking on, I would be bringing shame onto myself and that shame would extend to my entire family. Our dignity was just about all we had, so when my father said, "Don't make a fool of yourself," he was laying a heavy weight on my seventeen-year-old shoulders.

So I squared up to the job and, with the help of Shorty, I did it right. But I never forgot the look on my father's face or the tone in his voice that day. Any time I had to face up to a challenge, the memory would come back to me. And I would do my best to act in a way that would preserve our dignity.

My father's warning was one of the first things that went through my mind after I had looked at Sandy McCurrach's telegram a second time, and also for a second time had said, "Who, me?" If it had just been Sandy's idea, I would have followed by saying, "Forget it." But there were other people around Kamloops with the same idea.

Nick Kalyk, an old friend from UBC Aggie days who went on to teach mathematics at Kamloops High, called several times in the next few days: he'd been talking to people about getting me to run, and the reaction was enthusiastic. He called a number of times to report progress, but for some reason, Nick couldn't seem to get it straight whether Ottawa was three hours ahead or behind Kamloops time, so he would often call at two or three in the morning. Then I heard from Vic Cates, another old friend who was president of an organization called the Mika-Nika Club—it means "You and Me" in Chinook, the old trading language—a group of progressive minded Kamloops people who believed in reaching out to help the Indian community.

Donna and I sat down and talked about it. "Why not give it a try?" she said. The kids weren't in school yet, and we weren't tied down by any other obligations. Winning would mean staying in Ottawa, but she wouldn't mind that—her mother was in North Bay, only a few hours up the road, and her brother was a banker in Toronto. "We can do this," Donna said, and I agreed to go out west and hear for myself what people were saying.

Sandy McCurrach and George Calveley had arranged for me to attend an informal coffee party at the Highlander Restaurant in Kamloops. I thought it might draw a couple of dozen people, but when I walked in the place was packed with 150 Liberals. "Holy Smokes," I said to Sandy, "are they all here to see me?"

Sandy assured me that they weren't; there were other candidates in attendance. Then he guided me into the crowd. I shook more hands in the next hour than I normally shook in a year. They wanted me to give a speech, so I said a few words about being happy to be back after three years away, and told them a little about what I'd been doing in Ottawa. I was honoured by the attention and said so. Finally I told them I was looking at going for the nomination as Liberal candidate, and that if I did so I would work for cleaner, more open government—the smell of the Munsinger Affair was still in the air in those days—and that I would try to make things better for my people. It was an all-white crowd, but I got a good response.

So back I went to Ottawa and talked seriously with Donna. I'd been bowled over by all the support at the coffee party—the words, "Who, me?" still kept ringing faintly somewhere in the back of my mind—but I didn't intend to let my hopes get high. For one thing, there were two other contestants for the Liberal nomination: Jack Chilton, the former mayor of North Kamloops, was a well-known name around town and no slouch when it came to putting together a campaign; even more intimidating was Peter Pearse, then just beginning a career that would make him BC's most celebrated resource economist, but already with a Rhodes Scholarship behind him. Also behind Pearse was Jarl Whist, former Liberal standard-bearer, big-gun lawyer and a local power in the party.

And, even if I could overcome the competition for the nomination, that would have been just the preliminary bout. The main fight would put me up against Davie Fulton, the biggest Tory west of the Rockies. Fulton controlled the riding: he had the papers behind him, as well as the business community and anybody who was anybody in Kamloops, including Indians—one of his nominators was Chief Clarence Jules Sr. of the Kamloops Band. I didn't see myself as just a sacrificial lamb, but I didn't expect to take Kamloops away from Davie Fulton. If I got the nomination, I would put up a good fight and say a few things on behalf of my people. I would not make a fool of myself.

The first person I called was my boss, Art Laing. He was very pleased. He was cleaning up some last minute things at his Ottawa office, before heading out to Vancouver to fight for re-election, but he offered to come up to Kamloops once the campaign got rolling. Later, I took him up on that offer, and he was the first Liberal heavy-hitter to come to the riding and give me his endorsement. The next person I called was Syd Smith, the Liberal Senator from Kamloops who was Speaker of the Senate. It was a little late in the evening when I got him on the phone, and he was already in his pajamas and robe, preparing for bed. But he had his driver bring him over so that he could be the first person to give me one hundred dollars toward the campaign.

I told Sandy McCurrach and George Calveley, and they started making calls and drawing other people in. Donna and the kids and I flew out from Ottawa, and we bunked in with the McCurrachs until we saw which way the nomination went.

I was invited to more coffee parties, small gatherings of a dozen or so people at Liberal supporters' homes. I was glad I wasn't having to start off by addressing large meetings; my experience as a square dance caller, augmented by a few months with the Kamloops Toastmasters Club, didn't make me any threat to Winston Churchill's reputation as the best political orator of the century. But standing in somebody's living room with a cup of coffee in my hand, I could do a pretty convincing impression of a politician. And, after a while, it started to come more naturally to me.

The word filtering back to me from my volunteer campaigners was that I was making a good impact. There was a groundswell building behind me among the existing rank-and-file Liberal members, and a lot of people were taking out memberships so that they could come and support me at the nominating convention. A few days before that meeting, Jack Chilton and Peter Pearse dropped out of contention—it was going to be an acclamation. I had to wonder whether all my supporters saw something in me that I didn't recognize in myself.

The only politician who had ever suggested that I run was Eugene Whelan, then a backbench MP. But he made the same suggestion to all minister's assistants. "You're chicken," was his standard line. "You have all this power borrowed from your ministers, but you never put yourself at the mercy of the people. If you had any balls, you'd go seek a nomination and run!"

The nominating convention was held on May 11 at the Kamloops Yacht Club, down on the Thompson River. It was a big hall with a small raised dais at one end, and about three hundred enthusiastic party members turned up, which my friends told me was not a bad turnout for an acclamation. There was no hoopla, though, just a few Trudeau posters on the walls and some Marchand buttons on people's lapels. The low-key image wasn't deliberate—I hadn't organized a campaign team yet, and there wasn't any money.

I was nominated by my old friend Gus Gottfriedsen, a successful rancher and a member of the Kamloops Band. The seconder was Bill Brennan, a local accountant who was the grand old man of the Liberal Party in Kamloops. He had been active in the party during the Mackenzie-King era, but his Liberal roots went even deeper: as a young man he had shaken hands with Sir Wilfrid Laurier. I relied on him often for sound advice and wisdom.

Grant Deachman, the MP for Vancouver Quadra, was our guest speaker, and he gave a barn burner on national unity and how British Columbians had to step up and take hold of our rightful place in Confederation. Naturally, he felt that the best way to do that was to elect more Liberal MPs who would go into the next Parliament under our exciting new leader and make BC's presence felt. Since he was talking to a room full of deeply committed Liberals, he got a rousing response.

Then it was my turn. And it was a good thing this was a nomination by acclamation, because if I'd had to win it by the quality of what I said and how I said it, I would have been in trouble. But I promised to do my best and to try to be worthy of the trust they were putting in me. Fortunately, Grant Deachman had wound them up so thoroughly that we went out of there still on a high.

Now that the campaign was on, we moved into a two bedroom townhouse in Kamloops's first condo development-people called them the "Rabbit Hutches"—on Pemberton Terrace near the radio station. People lent us everything we would need—beds, furniture, dishes and so on—and a young woman named Linda Martin, eighteen years old and just out of high school, the daughter of a Liberal doctor and a Tory mother, volunteered to look after Lennie and Lori, so Donna and I could be free to campaign full-time. Linda, though young, had strong opinions about child-rearing—she believed that kids should be part of whatever their parents were doing—and would suddenly appear with our little ones at campaign events. It didn't seem to do them any harm.

I asked Jarl Whist, who had championed Peter Pearse's bid for the nomination, to be campaign chairman. He left his law practice in the hands of his partners—one of whom was Rafe Mair, future Socred cabinet minister and radio hotliner—and immediately threw himself into the job of getting me elected. Jarl was a canny old pro, having been a candidate himself, and he adapted very quickly to the new style of campaign that suddenly arrived when Trudeaumania ignited politics in Canada.

But, in the opening days of the Kamloops campaign, Trudeaumania was still in the egg. Figuring, wisely, that I was not the kind of candidate to wow the electorate at big events, Jarl kept me going to little coffee parties at supporters' homes; I would attend four or five a day—a total of maybe 125 for the campaign—never making a speech, but just talking quietly with people about the issues they considered important. These days, we keep being told that what people really care about is economics—taxes, exchange rates and unemployment statistics mostly—but in the late sixties, most ordinary Canadians had a broader view of things. The people I talked to were concerned about big issues: they looked south at the riots and protest marches, and they wondered what kind of society we ought to be building up here in our half of North America; they looked at the unrest in Québec, and worried about continuing to have a country in which to build at all.

My constant companion was Mack Bryson, a rancher and former Aggie who later taught high school. He was my driver and general factotum for the campaign, slow-talking, level-headed and utterly dependable. He would pick me up at the Rabbit Hutches early every morning and deliver me back, usually groggy from a whole day of talking and travelling and handshaking. Years later, when he worked in my Kamloops office, my Ottawa ministerial staff referred to him as "Marshall Bryson," because he came across as the kind of unflappable straight-arrow that Gary Cooper used to play. I was always glad to have him with me when the campaign staff pressured me into attending an all-candidates meeting.

Kamloops-Cariboo was a big riding in those days, all the way from Hixon and Quesnel up in the Cariboo down to Merritt in the South, from Canoe in the east to Cache Creek in the west. To get me around, the campaign rented a little Cessna, piloted by Dick Kelly. It wasn't until after election day that we learned that our pilot had only recently qualified to fly solo. The hours he spent in the air, moving me from one small airstrip to another, allowed him to qualify for his full licence.

I had never been involved in an election campaign before, so I was learning as I went along. Fortunately, although I didn't at first realize it, I was getting a very gentle introduction to the political arena—things couldn't have gone better. There was intense interest in the election among ordinary people. Even in small-towns like Hixon and Clinton, forty or fifty people would turn out to hear the candidates speak. Normally, the seats at all-candidates meetings are filled by campaign workers and hard-line party activists, but in the summer of 1968 a lot of Canadians had taken the concept of participatory democracy to heart.

An early inkling of the way things were heading came at an all-candidates meeting in Salmon Arm, which was always the most pro-Conservative region of the riding. For most of the voters there, Davie Fulton could do no wrong. If he had walked to the meeting across the waves of the arm of Shuswap Lake that gives the town its name, they wouldn't have been much surprised.

All of us candidates were sitting behind a table at the front of the high school gymnasium, the place packed to standing-room only. We were answering questions posed by a moderator, passing along the single microphone when we had had our allotted turn. I was the last candidate to answer a particular question—I can't remember what it was—and was handing the mike back to the moderator, when Fulton decided he wanted to add something to the remarks he had already made. As he reached to intercept the microphone, there was a disapproving rumble from the crowd. Somebody called out, "You've had your turn!"

It was a little thing, but it seemed to me that if Davie Fulton couldn't use the home-court advantage in Salmon Arm, then we just might have a better chance than we had thought of taking this long-time Tory riding. Later, I said as much to Jarl Whist, causing the old campaigner to roll his eyes and mutter something to the effect that he'd have to check his Bible, but he was pretty sure that if Salmon Arm ever went Liberal it would be one of the seven signs of the Apocalypse.

Still, the campaign kept picking up momentum from somewhere. Fresh volunteers came in every day, many of them young, most of them getting involved in politics for the first time. One was Jim Davidson, a university student who had come home to Blue River for the summer, and who lived and breathed politics even though he was too young to vote. A few years later, he would be on my ministerial staff as a political assistant. Eventually, we had more than 2,300 workers, far more than we could find jobs for. The same kind of thing was happening all over Canada; it was as if the whole country wanted to be part of what was happening.

Nowadays when so many people get so excited, the cause is usually a sports tournament or the release of a new Star Wars movie, with millions of dollars being spent to generate hype that will pay off at the box office. But in 1968, we still thought of ourselves as citizens of a country, not consumers in a global market. The fervour came out of Canadians themselves. In the days before Margaret Thatcher, Ronald Reagan and Brian Mulroney, government was not seen as a hindrance to the happiness of the commons, a necessary evil to be kept as small and ineffectual as possible. We believed that government was an embodiment of ourselves; it was how "we the people" expressed our collective will. Government was an instrument that we Canadians could put our hands on. We would use it to reshape our society, to make our country reflect all the new hopes and energies of our second century.

Millions of us focused those hopes and energies on Pierre Elliott Trudeau. The Americans had had John F. Kennedy, the British had the Beatles, and now we Canadians would have our own symbol of how the times they were a'changing. To honour our first hundred years, we had gone out and covered the landscape with commemorative private and public works—everything from new hockey arenas to the mass biffie burning in some little town in Manitoba. Now 1967 was over, but we still felt like celebrating. Putting Pierre Trudeau in the prime minister's office would be our last great centennial project.

But there was also a dark side to Trudeaumania. Canada had had years of FLQ bombs in mailboxes: ordinary people had been suddenly and violently blown out of their lives. The two solitudes of English and French Canada were so distant from each other that we might as well have been on different hemispheres of the planet, instead of sharing the same stretch of geography for a hundred years. In Kamloops and in many other parts of Canada, there was a feeling that French Canadians—we didn't call them Québecers in those days—were out to spoil the party for all of us. Many westerners thought that Canada needed somebody who could "put Québec in its place," and Trudeau was supposed to be that somebody.

Boy, did they pick the wrong guy. If there was one thing Pierre Trudeau cared about, it was people's rights. French Canadians paid taxes like any other Canadians; they were citizens like everybody else, and they had a right to participate in their country. Trudeau meant to see that those rights were upheld.

As an Indian, I knew what it was like to be born into a country you weren't allowed to be fully part of. And when I went to Ottawa, I soon saw the same kind of double-standard being applied to French Canadians. I met a lot of them around the House of Commons—but they were porters and cafeteria staff and drivers. There were very few francophone deputy ministers; they were all mostly anglophones, and scarcely any of them could speak more than schoolboy French. It was pretty obvious that if your name was Yves or André and you wanted a career in the public service of Canada, you had to set your sights low and resign yourself to finishing no better than the middle of the pack; no matter how capable you were, the top jobs went to English Canadians.

That was wrong. More than that, as Trudeau saw it, if French Canadians could not participate equally in the country they had helped build, it was no wonder that many of them were talking about taking Québec out of Canada, so that they would be masters in their own home. Trudeau's solution—and Lester Pearson's before him—was to make French Canadians feel at home in Canada by making the country officially bilingual.

I spent years listening to people telling me that Trudeau was out to "shove French down our throats." Some of them were misinformed; some of them were simply bigots. But nobody ever forced

Donna pinning a rose on Pierre Trudeau on his visit to Kamloops during the 1968 election campaign.

anybody to learn French. They just had to be willing to let their fellow Canadians feel comfortable in their own country, at least to the extent offered by a bilingual sign in a Kamloops post office. It's because so many English-speaking Canadians couldn't allow that minimum of grace to French Canadians that we have a separatist government in Québec and a separatist party in the House of Commons. But all of that was far in the future in the summer of 1968, when most of the country was turning Pierre Trudeau into a blank screen onto which they could project their hopes and dreams.

He came to Kamloops on June 3, a little more than three weeks before election day. We'd seen the news about the big crowds and the mounting enthusiasm down in Vancouver and Victoria, but we weren't expecting much of that in Kamloops. Gordon Smith, Senator Syd Smith's son, took Donna and me out to the airport in his old white Cadillac convertible, and we drove into pure bedlam.

Nick Kalyk was our campaign strategist for rallies and parades, and he had created a corps of "Trudeau Girls," fifty teenagers in orange miniskirts and beanies—remember, this was before feminism

Trudeau Girls waiting for Pierre Trudeau's plane to land at the Kamloops airport, Election campaign 1968.

and political correctness—and they were dancing around on the tarmac screaming "Marchand!" and "Trudeau!" like cheerleaders at a high school pep rally. Behind the girls, though, the terminal was crammed with people; the windows were packed with them and the gate leading into the building was a solid mass of sightseers. When Trudeau's chartered DC-9 came down the runway and taxied over to the apron, the spectators went wild, clapping, cheering, whistling, jostling for a better view.

I guess the Prime Minister was starting to get used to it by then, but it was a little unnerving for Donna and me. We introduced him to the campaign workers who were there and to the Trudeau Girls— some of them looked as if they'd just shaken hands with all four of the Beatles—and all the time, the crowd kept cheering in the background. Then we climbed into the back seat of the Cadillac for the ride into Kamloops.

The airport was pretty far out of town in those days, past sparsely populated Brocklehurst, but we weren't more than a few hundred meters out of the gate before we saw people standing on the side of the road. They waved, and we waved back. A few meters on, there was another group. Trudeau said, "Let's sit up," so he and Donna and I perched ourselves on the top of the back seat, and from there all the way into the city, the road was lined with smiling, waving people.

We drove to the front door of the North Kamloops sports centre. Nick Kalyk had said to expect a good crowd: he and two hundred volunteers had gone door-to-door all over town, hand-delivering invitations to come and have beef-on-a-bun with Trudeau and Marchand. But when we climbed the stairs onto a balcony overlooking the playing field, we were looking at a sea of humanity. The news media estimated that we had drawn up to nine thousand people from a community of thirty thousand; most of the voters of Kamloops were on the field waiting to meet Pierre Trudeau. The cooks had already run out of beef and switched to hamburgers; when they ran dry on hamburgers, they'd fallen back on hot dogs, and by the time we arrived, the hot dogs were almost gone.

I introduced Trudeau and he said a few words to the crowd. It was a short speech about the need for the country to have vision and to

Pierre addressing the crowd of 9,000 at the campaign rally in Kamloops 1968.

pull ourselves together. As he always did, he added a few words in French, and the people cheered. Then he turned to me and said, "Imagine this kind of rally in Davie Fulton's back yard. I think you're going to win." I glanced over at Jarl Whist on the other side of the PM; he looked like a man searching for a piece of wood to knock on.

We followed Trudeau down into the field. Political leaders in those days didn't need the kind of heavy-duty bodyguard protection they get today. The boss was attended by a couple of plainclothes Mounties, and the campaign had asked some big local guys, like six-foot-two-inch Ernie Klapstock, to try to run interference, but they were just swamped. People were pushing in, offering their hands to be shaken, wanting to pat Trudeau's shoulder, or just to touch him as he went by. They crowded so tightly around Gordon Smith's Cadillac when it was time to take the PM back to the hotel that they dented the bodywork. I've never seen anything like it, before or since. It was exciting. It was scary.

If I had been thinking about the future, I might have wondered if any human being could live up to the expectations that were on the beaming faces and in the chattering voices of all those people. Certainly, Pierre Trudeau wouldn't—and couldn't have. But no thoughts like those were on my mind that evening in Kamloops; I was thinking about the immediate future, because it was becoming clear that I might very well win the election. The next day, after we had seen the PM back to his plane and gone back to our rabbit hutch, I said to Donna, "Looks like I'm going to be a politician."

She said, "Well, I guess I'll have to be a politician's wife." She was an enthusiastic campaigner and followed our PR advisor's counsel to always smile and wave to people on the street. One day, that advice almost got her into trouble. Our campaign headquarters were at the back of the Central Hotel, which had a reputation for attracting women who were known to wave at men for non-electoral purposes. We were coming out of headquarters to go have lunch with Liberal lawyer Merv Chertkow and his wife Jean, when a young man drove up to the curb and smiled at Donna. She smiled and waved back, very friendly, and the young man beckoned her over to the car.

"Get in," he said. "I can't stop here."

She jumped in the car and they drove off, but they hadn't gone far before Donna discovered that the fellow's focus of interest was not on her politics. When she declined his offer and explained why, he said he was disappointed, but he gallantly drove her back to where he had picked her up. Donna told me afterwards, "There's a lot of things I'll do to win a vote for you, dear, but I've got to draw the line somewhere."

After Trudeau's visit, I thought we had it won. We spent the next three weeks trying not to make some dumb mistake that would cancel the magic spell. Then came Election Day, which is always a curious time for a candidate. There is nothing more that can be done; you're in the hands of the voters, and all you can do is cast your own ballot and wait till the polls close at eight p.m. I went around to the polls with Jarl Whist to thank the workers for all their efforts, then we hunkered down in our condo to see how it would go. Donna said she would be disappointed if I didn't win, but that she would feel sorry for Davie Fulton if I did.

Our election night headquarters was at a big room in the Plaza Hotel. People started arriving early, and more kept coming in until the room was hot and loud. We had all the polls listed on big sheets of paper tacked to the walls, and people with markers ready to mark down the results as the count was phoned in from the polling stations. By 8:15, the first calls were coming in. We won a poll, then another poll, then one from North Kamloops, and that was significant because that was the NDP stronghold. With each poll won, there were cheers from the crowd of workers and supporters. Caps were coming off the brown stubby beer bottles and corks were coming out of the wine bottles. People were starting to say, "We're going to win."

Jarl Whist was still knocking on wood. He remembered campaigns when he'd been solidly ahead until the results came in from Salmon Arm, a flood of Tory votes that gave the election to Davie Fulton. At 8:25, the CBC declared me a winner and Pierre Trudeau called to congratulate us. Jarl took the call and asked the PM to phone back later; he wasn't prepared to accept victory until he saw what Salmon Arm was doing. Eventually, those polls came in, and—Trudeaumania or no Trudeaumania—Salmon Arm kept faith with the

Election Night 1968 Davie Fulton, always the gentleman, conceding defeat and congratulating us on our victory and good campaign.

Tory candidate, though not by enough votes to keep Davie Fulton in his House of Commons seat. I sometimes wonder if, years later, Pierre remembered that Salmon Arm never went Liberal when he looked through his train window at the protesters on the station platform, and raised one finger in what British Columbians now refer to as the "Salmon Arm salute."

But on election night in 1968, the Prime Minister dutifully called back again at ten o'clock and congratulated me. I was touched that Davie Fulton, ever the gentleman, came to the Plaza to shake my hand. He then raised my arm in victory for the photographers, and the picture made the front page of the next day's Kamloops *Sentinel* and also ran in the *Vancouver Sun*.

We went off to Mack and Liz Bryson's for a celebratory bash, and things got moderately wild. There was a pool and I remember people jumping into it including our finance chair, the prominent local lawyer Don Andrews in his new suit, as well as a strikingly attractive woman schoolteacher from Merritt whose students would probably have been surprised to see her splashing around in a red bra and panties.

At 5:30 in the morning, Donna and I walked hand in hand up the hill to our townhouse. The final tally showed that I had received exactly 13,000 votes. Canada was about to turn 101, British Columbia had been part of Confederation for ninety-three years, and that's how long it had taken for an Indian to have a voice as a Member of Parliament. I thought about my North American Indian Brotherhood Days when George Manuel and the other leaders would talk about how much it would mean once we had the vote. Now it was a dozen years later, and one of us was an MP. I didn't realize that more than thirty years after that election night, I would still be the only BC Indian ever elected to the Commons.

I also thought about the time when I had broken the law of Canada by voting in the election of 1958. I was still at UBC then, and living at a boarding house on West Thirteenth run by Mabel (Binky) Reid, the ex-wife of Haida artist Bill Reid. When the enumerators came around, Binky put me on the voters list, and on election day I went down to the polling station, marked a ballot and put it in the box. It was a conscious and deliberate criminal act, and I sweated bullets afterwards, thinking, "What if it's a controversial election and they review the voters' list and find out that this little Indian illegally cast a ballot? I could go to jail."

I didn't feel good about voting illegally, nor about the time I bought a bottle of rye, contrary to the law of Canada. I didn't think that I was getting away with something; I felt that I was taking a risk to do the right thing. Many Indians felt that way in those days: that it was our duty to break the unjust laws that forbade us to do this or that because of the colour of our skins. Those bad laws made us into lawbreakers; we couldn't be anything else and still live with ourselves. That is what discriminatory laws teach to those they discriminate against.

I had my first test as a politician about three hours after we got to bed after the election night party. About 8:30 in the morning, there

was a pounding on the door of our condo. I got up, not feeling exactly one hundred per cent, to find on my doorstep three men in their
thirties, dressed in jeans and raggedy tee-shirts and worn-out shoes.
They wanted to know if I was the guy who got elected. When I said
yes, one of them said, "You said you wanted to help poor people.
Well, we could use some help."

At first I thought they were putting me on. But we talked a little,
and it became clear to me that they honestly expected me to arrange
jobs for them or, failing that, give them some kind of hand-out. They
figured that was what a Member of Parliament did for a living.
Politely, even though I was feeling the effects of a strenuous campaign, a big party and three hours sleep, I straightened them out and
sent them down to Canada Manpower.

But I thought about it afterwards: these three guys were about my
age, we came from the same part of the world, yet they didn't have a
clue about how their country was governed. They were from that big
chunk of the population that doesn't know the difference between a
municipal councillor, a member of a provincial legislature or a federal
MP. For them, government was just a vague blur somewhere off in the
distance. Probably all the fuss on TV about Trudeaumania had got
them interested in politics for the first time. It didn't occur to me
then, though maybe it should have, that Pierre's plans to involve the
whole population of Canada in participatory democracy might have
overlooked what the example of those three young men said about
the way Canadians expected to be governed.

Later that day, when I'd had a little more sleep, we drove down to
Six Mile Creek and visited with my parents and my brother Ray. We
have never been a huggy-kissy family, and we don't feel it's dignified
to brag when we've done something significant, but it was easy to tell
how proud my mom and dad were that their son was Canada's first
Indian MP. We spent the day just sitting and visiting with family and
friends. Lori and Len Jr. took turns riding my dad's only gentle horse
around the pasture.

I also received a touching telegram from Henry Castillou. It said,
"I am so proud of you, it is as if I had sired a son."

I spent the next couple of weeks in the riding. We had rallies and parties and get-togethers large and small to thank all the hundreds of workers who had made the campaign happen. One of these events was very special to me: Ernest Brewer, the chief of my home reserve, hosted a special picnic at Round Lake. More than three hundred people—my immediate family, as well as uncles, aunts, cousins and friends, amounting to half the population of the reserve—gathered to celebrate. There were no celebrities or visiting bigwigs, just us Indians coming together to take note that, this time, one of the lobsters had made it out of the bucket.

The media had noticed that something unusual had happened in Kamloops-Cariboo. Sheldon Turcott from CBC came up to the riding with a film crew for a feature interview which later ran on the national news. We talked on my friend Gus Gottfriedsen's ranch, me looking parliamentary in a suit and tie. When we got around to my background as a cowboy, Sheldon noticed a saddled horse grazing nearby. "Can you really ride?" he asked. I was new to the art of being interviewed in those days, and I guess I figured it would be kind of a novelty for a new MP to be seen on horseback. So I climbed up on Gus's horse in my city suit and showed Sheldon a few moves. I'm just glad he didn't ask me to do any rope tricks.

Not many reporters knew much about Indians in those days. Nowadays because of Oka and the stand-off at Gustafsen Lake, because of treaty talks in British Columbia and the dispute over fishing rights in the Maritimes, Indians are in the news all the time. But in the late sixties, we were still Canada's forgotten people. Most reporters and editors knew very little about us, and a lot of what they did know was wrong. In my first few weeks as an MP, I attracted a fair amount of media attention and had to field a lot of questions based on the usual false stereotypes. Once again, there was that unthinking assumption that, if one of us was getting somewhere, it had to be a case of tokenism.

To be fair, there were some knowledgeable reporters around, who had taken the trouble to background themselves on our issues. Ron Rose at the *Vancouver Sun* was writing some good stuff about us; he genuinely cared about Indians. Stu Lake, the Canadian Press bureau chief in Ottawa, knew what he was writing about. So did Terry

Hargreaves, who headed up CBC radio's Ottawa bureau.

I admit it was gratifying to be one of the flavours of the month. I did *Canada AM* with Charles Lynch, the dean of political columnists, who was good to me and didn't try to trip me up, as he often did with politicians. He had the advantage of knowing more about what was going on in Ottawa than just about anybody else. Along with Lincoln Alexander, Canada's first black MP and later Lieutenant Governor of Ontario, I was interviewed for a big feature article in the *Canadian Weekend* magazine on racism in Canada.

I was an easy story, and luckily nobody savaged me. I just kept saying the same thing: that Indians were just the same as any other Canadians, and that more of us should get involved in the country's public life. After a while, it seemed to me that I had nothing new to say, and I began turning down interview requests. That was a rookie's mistake. I didn't realize that there is no such thing as too much publicity in politics, nor that responding to the same old questions with the same old answers is part of the game. The media expect consistency: change your mind, even on the best evidence, and the knee-jerk media reaction is to accuse you of flip-flopping. Reporters like politicians who fit easily into ready-made categories. Politicians who think and evolve give the media trouble.

Early on in my career, there was one occasion when I did tread close to the stereotype. After Christmas, 1968 I was flying home to Kamloops to attend the funeral of my cousin Berneice and had to change planes in Toronto. The airport was undergoing some construction, and we passengers had to walk across the tarmac in blowing sleet to climb the mobile staircase and board the DC-8. I was carrying under my arm a shallow cardboard box about four feet long and a foot wide and when I got to the top of the stairs the stewardess stopped me and said, "Excuse me, sir, is there a gun in that box?"

I said, quite truthfully, "No, it's a bow and arrow."

She looked at me, looked at the box, then grabbed it and held up the entire line of cold, windblown passengers while she tore it open. It contained a toy bow and arrow that belonged to George Calveley's young son. They had been visiting us for Christmas and had left it behind.

The stewardess handed the box back with a blush of embarrassment and a profuse apology. She was extra attentive to me all the way out to Vancouver.

In mid-July Donna and the kids and I came back to Ottawa on the SuperContinental. My MP's rail pass allowed us all to ride for free, but eating and sleeping were our own concern, so we paid extra for two sleepers. We moved back into our Bayshore townhouse, and I reported to the Speaker's Office on Parliament Hill to find out where my office would be. I was assigned to 133S in the Centre Block.

It's always an honour to be chosen by the people to be their representative, but in the late sixties that prominence was not accompanied by luxurious accommodations or high rates of pay. As an assistant to Art Laing, I had had my own relatively spacious office in one of Robert Campeau's buildings. My secretary had had her own office.

Being sworn in as a new M.P. July 1968 by Alastair Fraser, clerk of the House of Commons, with Donna, Len Jr. and Lori Anne.

As an MP, I shared one small room with Marg Mellor, my new secretary. I also took a $1,000 cut in pay, which when you consider that an MP's salary in 1968 was only $12,000 a year, made for a noticeable reduction in the size of my paycheque.

I would also be working harder. Most Canadians think an MP's job is to sit in the House of Commons chamber and debate legislation. That may have been the case back before my time, when government was a remote and distant part of most people's daily life, and most citizens could justifiably claim that the only time they heard from their Member of Parliament was at election time when the MP came around looking for votes. But things were changing in the late 1960s. Government was becoming activist, and people's lives were being touched by the growing number of programs—CPP, Medicare, job creation schemes, new immigration rules—and there was a growing sense that government was everybody's business.

More and more, an MP's day was being taken up with directly helping constituents—so maybe those three guys on my Kamloops doorstep weren't completely wrong. Any of the 80,000 people in my riding were entitled to call on my help in dealing with any federal government matter: passports, pensions, UIC claims, citizenship, veterans' benefits, immigration, Indian affairs. And, since it is not unheard of for people to get themselves wrapped up in bureaucracy to the point of being paralyzed, there were a lot of complaints and requests for assistance coming over an MP's desk. Every mail delivery brought a fresh supply.

Later, as a result of lobbying by MPs of all parties, funds were allocated for extra staff in the House of Commons and for staffed offices in the constituencies, which made it possible for the elected members to deliver the level of service that participatory democracy requires. But, to begin with, it was just me and one very capable secretary. Despite the workload, I made it a policy to personally answer every piece of mail I received. I believe that sticking to that policy played a major role in my being re-elected twice. I was also greatly helped over the years by the skilful and dedicated staff in my Kamloops constituency office, especially Heather Allen, Roberta Derrick, Joan McNamee and Mack Bryson. I am grateful to them all.

Once Parliament sat, the work increased. Pierre Trudeau believed that the system of standing committees should be expanded and that their members—MPs from all parties—should be given more work to do. Detailed consideration of legislation that used to be undertaken in the House of Commons chamber would now be the work of the standing committees. And since the PM envisioned an ambitious legislative program for the new Parliament, there would be plenty of work for everybody. The House would sit from Monday through Friday, with evening sittings on Mondays, Tuesdays and Thursdays.

During the Mulroney years, the backbenchers' workload was eased, and the MPs were given regular weeks off to take care of constituency business and get away from the constant grind. But in Trudeau's time, it was hard work and plenty of it. Pierre may have had an early image as a playboy, but that was all a confection of the media, based on the fact that he drove a Mercedes sports car and dated glamorous women. Behind the image, Trudeau had an immense appetite for digging into a pile of work and getting it done, and he expected everybody around him to be the same.

My office in the Centre Block was right next door to Ray Perrault's and around the corner from Paul St. Pierre's. St. Pierre was the MP for Coast Chilcotin, a big riding that ran from the southern border of my constituency over the coastal mountains and down to the Sunshine Coast. He had a strong connection to the Cariboo: he had spent some time living in a cabin there; more important, he had been writing about the region for years, producing a number of books, one of which had been turned into a CBC TV series called *Cariboo Country*. One of the continuing cast members was a hereditary chief of the Burrard Band named Dan George, who had also had some small parts in Hollywood movies.

Two years later, in 1970, Chief Dan George became an international celebrity when he co-starred with Dustin Hoffman in the movie, *Little Big Man*. By then we had gotten to know each other quite well, through Paul St. Pierre, and he would use my office as a hideaway when he was in Ottawa. He was on the cocktail circuit a lot in those days, using his high profile to promote Indian causes, but he was well into his seventies and the press of attention from well-wishers and autograph seekers would sometimes wear him down. So he would come to my office and just hang out for a while, and sometimes I would drive him out to the airport or on to his next engagement.

Chief Dan George and I were responsible for one small change in Parliamentary tradition. It involved the parliamentary restaurant, which is like an old-fashioned, private gentlemen's club whose members are MPs, reporters accredited to the press gallery and two members of each minister's staff. Standards are very strict: no males are admitted unless they are properly dressed in jacket and tie. Early on in my time as an MP, I had invited guests up to lunch at the restaurant only to be embarrassed when we could not go in because my visitors were not appropriately dressed.

One evening, after Chief Dan George had spent most of the afternoon at my office, I invited him up to dinner. But he was dressed in a traditional ribbon shirt—a multi-coloured shirt with ribbons sewn to the shoulders—and a beaded neckpiece. Those qualify as formal dress among his people, but I was worried that the Parliamentary restaurant staff might have other ideas. I had learned from my earlier mistake and now kept a spare jacket and tie in the office, but it would have looked pretty silly to have made my friend put them on over his Indian clothes. So I went up ahead of him, asking him to wait in the office while I went and spoke to the maître d'.

"Listen," I told her, "my friend Chief Dan George is coming in to have dinner with me. He's wearing the traditional formal dress of our people, and if I get a lot of lip from anybody here, I'm going to go down to the Speaker's Office and raise holy hell." Well, the air turned fairly frosty, but I went back down and brought Dan up, and we were seated without a word. I was never much for throwing my weight around, but I wasn't going to have that good and decent man turned away from the door because he wasn't wearing a white man's clothes. And from then on, traditional Indian dress was considered acceptable for parliamentary dining.

I was saddened at the passing of Chief Dan George in 1981. He was a deeply religious man, a member of the Catholic Legion of Mary. The dignity that he gave to his portrayal of "Old Lodge Skins," his character in *Little Big Man*, probably did more to restore the stature of our people among white society than the efforts of any Indian politician, including this one.

Not too long after I had settled into my cramped office on Parliament Hill and was discovering just how much work an MP has to do, I received a phone call from the Prime Minister's Office, asking me to be available to take a call from Pierre Trudeau himself. At the appointed time, the PM called. I'd had time to think about what he might want of me—I didn't expect to be asked into the Cabinet—so I was not surprised when he said that he wanted me to second the Address in Reply to the Speech From the Throne when the new session of Parliament convened. I was ready with my reply, and therefore did not say, "Who, me?" to the PM; I said, "You bet."

Whenever the House of Commons sits for a new session, the government presents its legislative intentions in the form of an address by the Governor-General to the combined membership of the Commons and the Senate—the Speech From the Throne—the content of which is subsequently debated in the Commons. To begin the debate, one Member of Parliament from the government side of the House moves acceptance of the Speech, and another MP from the government backbench seconds the motion. It is traditional that one of these two MPs comes from the east, and the other from the west. It is also the custom that each will be a newly elected member of the House, giving his very first address in Parliament.

Now, anyone who has been to Ottawa and sat in the visitor's gallery will know that most MPs' speeches are given to, at most, two or three dozen other members—enough to form a quorum and keep the place in session. But the debate on the Speech From the Throne is one of those high and mighty occasions when everybody shows up. So, although I gladly said, "You bet," to Pierre, I had to recognize that my debut—which would also be my people's—in the Parliament of Canada was not going to be a low-key affair. There would be ample opportunity to make a fool of myself.

I had a few days to prepare and went to the archives for some examples of what others had done before me. I talked to Art Laing and got some good advice. Then I sat down and laid out a framework and began to put together some remarks. After a couple or three attempts, I had to admit to myself that, though I would have been okay if I'd been writing a paper for a scientific journal, I was not a gifted speech writer. Fortunately, I knew someone who was. His name was Bill Fox, a Vancouver writer who had been brought into Indian Affairs by Art Laing, who lived not far from us in Bayshore. I gave him a call and he came right over, took away my scribblings, and came back the next day with a wonderful draft. We fiddled with it a little, and then I went with it.

On September 13, 1968, I was in my seat far down the government side of the Chamber, only a few places from the big doors through which the Mace is ceremonially carried. Lucien Lamoureux, the first person to be elected to the Speaker's position by the Members of the House, was in his great chair. Down to my left was Pierre Trudeau, surrounded by the heavyweights of the cabinet. Across from him was Bob Stanfield, the Leader of the Opposition, and seated a little farther back and to his right was John Diefenbaker. Almost directly across the aisle from me was David Lewis, leader of the NDP and Réal Caouette, leader of the Creditistes.

The debate had been opened by Eymard Corbin, an MP from New Brunswick who remains a good friend to this day. He wound up his speech and sat down to a sound like thunder, as MPs pounded their fists on the hardwood tops of their desks—this was before television coverage of Parliament prompted MPs to express their approval by the more dignified method of polite applause. The Speaker turned to me and said, "The Honourable Member for Kamloops-Cariboo." I rose in my place, and all those faces turned toward me.

Bud Orange, an MP from the Northwest Territories, had told me, "Remember, these guys—Trudeau, Diefenbaker—they all put their pants on one leg at a time," but I was more than a little nervous. My nerves weren't just because I was personally shy: this was the first time, in all the centuries since the Europeans had begun arriving in what would one day become the Dominion of Canada, that any of us, the original inhabitants, had had the right to stand up in the centre of government and speak. Whatever I might think of my own

Going to the Senate to hear the Speech from the Throne, Sept 1968,
with Eymard Corbin, MP Madawaska—Victoria, NB (ahead),
Robert Thompson MP Red Deer, Alta., Hon Walter Dinsdale, PC, MP,
Brandon-Souris, Man. and Bud Orange, MP, NWT (behind).

qualities, this was history, and it was all up to me.

I remembered what my father had said to me, back in that tomato field seventeen years before. I tried to think of John Diefenbaker
struggling into his trousers, then I opened my mouth and said, "Mr.
Speaker..."

I won't reproduce the entire speech here. There were certain formalities to be observed: I praised our new Speaker and our new Prime
Minister; I commended Davie Fulton as a great parliamentarian; I
spoke about my riding of Kamloops-Cariboo, about its resources and
communities, about the aspirations and problems of the people I was
elected to serve. And then I laid out the philosophy that would govern my actions as the first Indian elected to the Parliament of Canada.

"I am the first Indian to sit as a member in this house, and I am con-
scious of my responsibilities. I recognize that the people of Kamloops-Cariboo

did not send me here to represent only a segment of the population. I know I must strive on behalf of all my constituents. However, I have an obligation that I could not escape even if I wished to, and that is my obligation to my fellow Indians. I am an Indian who is a Member of Parliament. I am not just the Indian people's member, but I must speak as well on their behalf...

"*It is not important to the house that a member is, or is not, an Indian. It is not really important to the people of my riding whether I am an Indian or not. It is important to the Indian people to know that one of us can become a member. It is important for the younger Indians who are in school and at university to know that, with reasonable hope, they can aspire to become whatever they wish to become and are capable of becoming. It is important for all Canada to know that this is not a land of bigotry and prejudice. It is important for all Canadians to keep it that way.*

"*Although the Indian people once held all this land and now have but little of it, although the Indian was once the master of his environment and is no longer, it is less than helpful to repine for a past that is gone... No one can turn back the clock. The useful, the important and the right thing to do is to master the environment that is.*"

I believed that in 1968. I believe it now.

I did one other thing in that first House of Commons speech. I honoured a debt that all Canadian Indians owed to a man who was sitting on the other side of the House. I looked directly at John Diefenbaker when I said, "I must pay tribute to the right honourable gentleman who sits on the opposite side of the house and who is responsible for extending the right to vote to my fellow Indians and myself. This was a recognition of a people who needed to be recognized and who needed the assurance that they were not forgotten."

Diefenbaker smiled and nodded his head in acknowledgement. I knew he was touched by what I had said, and I was glad of it. Partisanship be damned, by giving us the vote, "the Chief" performed the single greatest act of benefit for our people since Canada was formed. Having the franchise meant that we were real human beings, no longer strangers in our own land.

When I finished, there was more desk thumping. The leaders of all parties came over to congratulate me, as is traditional. Diefenbaker also came and shook my hand, said, "Young man, that was very good," and later sent me a handwritten note to thank me for recognizing him. He wished me well and hoped I would be a good parliamentarian, and invited me to call on him if there was any help he could offer. I took the offer of mentorship as mere politeness and did not follow up on it—we were, after all, on different sides of the House. But not long after, following an interview on local CBC TV, the phone rang in my office and that instantly identifiable voice said, "John Diefenbaker here. Young man, I saw your interview last night and I want to give you one bit of advice. You spoke too quickly. Slow down a little. It will be more effective." It was good advice and I took it.

From time to time during my rookie years as an MP, Diefenbaker would stop me in the corridors of Parliament and offer me more tips on how to be a more effective MP. I was never sure exactly what motivated his kindness: it might have been because I was an Indian and he wanted to help my people; he might have felt that there was a bond between us because of my remarks in the Throne Speech debate; or he may have just been grateful that I had removed Davie Fulton from the Conservative caucus after Fulton had had the nerve to run against the Chief for the Tory leadership. It was probably a mixture of all three—John Diefenbaker was a complicated man.

The night of my first speech the Governor-General hosted the traditional gala for the opening of a new parliament. Donna and I drove there in our no-frills Biscayne and did our best to blend in with the glittering throng. Pierre Trudeau, still in his bachelor days, arrived with a stunning blonde who was the older sister of a TV star. The evening started out very formal, with an RCMP band in full red serge and spurs playing nothing more modern than a foxtrot. But after the Micheners retired early for the evening, Donna and I joined some of the younger MPs and their spouses—Maurice and Janet Foster, Keith and Mary Penner, Murray and Barbara McBride—in asking the Mounties to reach for a little rock and roll. What they produced may not have been quite what Buddy Holly and Carl Perkins had had in mind, all those years ago, but it had a beat and we could dance to it—which is what we kept on doing until dawn. Donna and I were among the last to leave Rideau Hall.

———

Making speeches in the Commons is probably the least frequent activity of a backbench Member of Parliament. One of the things that keeps an MP most busy is trying to get government to work for his constituency, but it sure helps if your seat is on the government side. In my first few weeks representing Kamloops-Cariboo, I was able to begin to repay the trust my constituents had placed in me.

The first project was a relatively small affair: the City of Merritt wanted to make some much needed improvements to the primitive little air strip outside of town—just some grading and paving and a small building where people could shelter from the weather while waiting for a plane. The mayor and council, with efforts from Davie Fulton, had been trying for years to get funding from the Canadian Ministry of Transport's Small Airports Program, but they couldn't get their application to the top of the pile. But now it was a new government and a new MP who didn't mind making a nuisance of himself if that was what it took; within a few weeks, I was handing Merritt's Mayor Allan Collette a federal cheque.

The other quick success of my early days ensured that the provincial fall fatstock show and the spring bull sale would take place in Kamloops as usual. The fall fair was an important part of the agricultural calendar—it was where the kids from 4-H showed their animals—and the bull sale was fundamental to the local cattle industry. The problem was that the buildings where the events always took place had burned down. The Kamloops Exhibition Association (KXA) was ready to rebuild on a piece of leased land across the river on the Indian Reserve, but they needed some funding to pay for the work.

I went to Bud Olson, the new Minister of Agriculture, and asked for some help. He was thinking of going to Cabinet for a $10 million global fund for agricultural infrastructure projects, but I knew the KXA couldn't wait. I asked Kamloops Mayor Peter Wing and Councillor Gordon Gamble, the chair of the committee that oversaw the Exhibition for the city council, to come down to Ottawa in a hurry. We managed to convince Bud Olson that the case was urgent, and came away with a $500,000 loan guarantee that enabled the KXA to be rehoused and ready when the bull sale came along.

Neither of these projects was a big deal in the history of Canada, or even of Kamloops-Cariboo, although they were important to the people involved. But they were important to me because they showed me that I could make a difference, and that I could do the job that the voters had sent me to Ottawa for.

Soon after we were sworn in as MPs, the Liberal House Leader asked each of us for a list of the Standing Committees we would like to serve on. I was young, full of energy and—unlike many MPs from Ontario and Québec—far enough away from my riding not to be visited by delegations of constituents every other day, so I asked to be given any and all work I could do. It was natural that I would be named to the Agriculture Committee: I was an agrologist representing a lot of ranchers. The Indian Affairs Committee was also a given. It soon became clear to the House Leader that I was a willing horse when it came to committee work, so I also worked on the Standing Committees on Broadcasting and on Resources and Public Works. I had particular reasons for wanting those assignments.

One reason that I wanted to get onto the broadcasting committee was so that I could help CTV realize its goal of establishing a broadcast tower in Kamloops. A lot of my constituents felt that they were being unfairly left out of things because there was no way to pick up the CTV signal. If you wanted to get Harvey Kirck's reading of the nightly news, you were out of luck. Eventually, the private broadcaster worked out an arrangement with local CBC affiliate CFJC to bring us CTV programs.

But getting CTV to come across for my constituents was a breeze compared to the battle to persuade CBC to bring its national AM radio programming to the people of Kamloops. People in smaller communities like Chase, Blue River and Cache Creek got a strong signal. Kamloops, one of the major cities of the BC Interior, got nothing but static. All we needed was a repeater station, consisting of a tower and a box of electronics that would pull the weak CBC signal out of the air and rebroadcast it strong and clear.

For the truly committed CBC radio listener, the need was desperate. There was one couple in Valleyview who loved to listen to the New York Philharmonic every Saturday morning. But the only way they could get their musical fix was to take a portable radio out across the road and under the telephone lines, which apparently acted as an antenna to draw in the CBC signal from Chase, 36 miles away. They would lie there in a drainage ditch, listening to Mozart and Tchaikovsky, and wondering why they weren't entitled to the national radio service their taxes were paying for.

I would put the same question to the CBC bigwigs, whenever they came before the Commons Standing Committee on Broadcasting to justify their existence. I never did get a straight answer. There were always technical difficulties, or a plan was in the works. But when all was said and done, it was a lot of saying and not much doing. And, since the CBC was a beloved national institution and not to be touched by mere politicians, there wasn't much more I could do than to make the Crown corporation's brass feel mildly uncomfortable for a while. In time, it became clear where the problem lay: the hierarchs at the CBC wanted to set up a full-scale broadcasting centre in our area with a broad range of regional programming. The fact that no AM signal was reaching the city strengthened their case; if they'd put in a repeater to bring in the national programming that Kamloops residents wanted, it would make it harder for the CBC mandarins to justify the much greater expense of opening a regional broadcasting centre. It was a conflict between what the citizens wanted and what the bureaucrats thought they should have, and it took five years of hammering away at the imperturbable CBC management before the people won and a repeater station went in.

I learned something from the experience, though. I learned that one of the most underestimated virtues in politics is simple persistence. Sure, you can do stunts and tricks for the news cameras, to make a short-lived splash—and all politicians have to do some of that from time to time. But the real work often gets done by people who keep saying the same thing, over and over, until the message gets through.

The thing that I did say, at least a hundred times in my first year as an MP, was that the proposal to divert water from the Shuswap watershed into Okanagan Lake was a recipe for ecological disaster. It was to fight the Shuswap Diversion that I had asked to be named to the Standing Committee on Resources and Public Works, because the plan to flush out polluted Okanagan Lake with water from the Shuswap system had been the biggest local issue in the election campaign. And I was dead against it.

So were the officials at the Inland Waters Directorate of the Department of Energy, Mines and Resources, headed by Jim Bruce, a highly capable civil servant who would later be my assistant deputy minister in the Environment department. Our problem was that the plan to divert massive amounts of water from one system to the other was the brainchild of the Government of British Columbia, which was led by the legendary W.A.C. Bennett, who just happened to represent the riding that included Okanagan Lake.

When I was growing up at Six Mile Creek, which fed into the Vernon Arm of Okanagan Lake, the water was clean and clear. But by the late 1960s, surrounded by a fast growing urban population and an expanding agricultural sector, Okanagan Lake was no longer the pristine body of water that public health and the increasingly important tourism industry required. Coliform levels were rising; oxygen-devouring algae blooms, fed by fertilizer residues carried into the lake by run-offs from orchards and vegetable farms, were killing fish. Something had to be done, and in those days, that meant calling in the engineers.

Today, when most Canadians have no trouble defining the word "ecology," the idea that anyone would arbitrarily divert one river basin into another is obviously a case of stepping on Mother Nature's bunions. But the 1960s were a different time. Engineers still ruled the earth, and to an engineer, just about anything that could be done should be done. That was the prevailing philosophy of the times, in government and in industry, and it explained why the Inland Waters Directorate was part of Energy, Mines and Resources, instead of the newly formed Environment department where it belonged.

In 1968, maybe one in a hundred people could define "ecology." I was one of those few because I was an agrologist who had done his master's thesis research on the ecology of sagebrush. But the word was starting to get tossed around. I once naughtily asked the head of a newly formed anti-pollution organization, a well-dressed and well-meaning society lady who had come to present a brief to the RPW Committee, if she could define the term. She had to lean over and conduct a whispered conversation with her hired consultant.

Because I knew what ecology meant, I knew that suddenly connecting together two entirely separate river basins meant mixing species that had never encountered each other before, each side carrying a full array of parasites and infectious diseases. As an Indian, I knew what would happen to the fish and crustaceans and plants in Okanagan Lake when their populations were abruptly hit by an invading army of germs they had never developed an immunity against. Measles and smallpox—not immigration—were the main reasons our people had ceased to be the majority in British Columbia, and had become a powerless remnant in a couple of generations.

"This is a dumb idea," I had said during the election campaign. Apart from the ecological stupidity of the plan, there was an economic threat to the people of the region. If the diversion lowered water levels in the Shuswap Lakes, it would reduce the attractiveness of some 1,100 miles of shoreline that were generating a lot of tourism revenues for the local economy. There were also questions about maintaining water levels for area ranchers who had to irrigate their hay crops with water from the Shuswap system. Most important of all, Little Shuswap Lake was a crucial stage on the great Adams River salmon run, and nobody knew what effects changing water levels—and therefore changing water temperatures—would have on one of the largest salmon stocks on the Pacific coast.

Before the election, a tough logger named Mike Riley, who lived on the north side of the Shuswap at Celista, had organized a group called the Shuswap Thompson River Research and Development Association (STRRADA), which represented thousands of my constituents opposed to the diversion. They expected me to fight for them, and I weighed in with every resource I could muster. The problem was this was primarily a provincial initiative, and the Province of

British Columbia under W.A.C. Bennett was no more happy to see the feds mixing into its plans than it is today under the NDP. Besides the inter-governmental tangle, there was the perennial problem of engineers hating to have their plans critiqued by any know-nothings from outside the profession. So the barricades were up and fully manned. Very little information was coming out of Victoria. I never did see a full, detailed plan for the project.

The obvious solution, and the one I was taking to Ottawa on behalf of my constituents, was to conduct a full study of the Okanagan River basin, lakes and all. We just didn't know enough about the water that was moving through the system, where the pollutants were coming from and how the problems could be addressed without resorting to the folly of connecting it up to another basin we also knew far too little about. It was like doctors proposing to transplant an organ from one person to another without either the donor or the recipient even getting a physical examination.

I pushed very hard to get the issue before the Standing Committee on Resources and Public Works, with help from Doug Stewart, the Liberal MP for Okanagan-Kootenay-Revelstoke. The committee was the best platform from which to generate some attention for the issue. We could call in experts from government and the academic community, get their concerns on the record and maybe educate the public and the Government of British Columbia on the dangers that lay ahead.

There was a statute on the books—the International River Improvements Act—which gave Ottawa some say on changes to any river that ran into the United States. The Okanagan River crossed the border just below Osoyoos. My ancestors had been travelling north and south along that river since long before there was a border. The Act gave us the legal lever we needed to lift the dead weight of the province's authority off the river. Through the committee, I pushed the federal Minister of Energy, Mines and Resources, Joe Greene, to commission a full federal-provincial study of the whole Okanagan basin. It took four years, and the scientists and technicians who conducted the study did a magnificent job. Their work demonstrated that no diversion was necessary; sophisticated environmental science, not brute strength engineering, would solve the problems of Okanagan Lake.

Halting the Shuswap Diversion was my first major victory, and I was given full credit even by the riding newspapers that had supported Davie Fulton. I learned a lot during that fight about how government really works—not about the highly visible process of public debate, but about the mundane mechanics of how files are pushed through levels of bureaucracy, until a decision is made. I was learning that the system works, but you have to know how to work the system.

Another issue that took several years of persistent effort to resolve was the fight to win equitable tax treatment for farm families that had incorporated their operations. One hand of government was encouraging farm families to incorporate because it was easier to do the accounting, while the other hand was penalizing incorporated family farms by not exempting them from capital gains tax when they passed from one generation to the next.

This was a big issue in cattle country. The late Gerard Guichon, from Quilchena, was chairing the Canadian Cattlemen's Association tax committee, and he and I spent years working on the problem. Every year during budget preparation time, he would come to Ottawa, and we would lobby the Minister of Finance: first it was John Turner, then Don McDonald, then Jean Chrétien. We would always be politely received and listened to, but eventually Gerard would get a letter that began, "We regret to inform you..."

The problem was a fear of the bureaucrats at the Finance Department that sharp-eyed tax lawyers for the big agricultural corporations would find some way to use the family farm exemption to hide large amounts of money from the taxman. But I am glad to say that, eventually, we wore them down. During debate on Jean Chrétien's first budget, when the House had gone into Committee of the Whole to debate the legislation, I got to my feet, ready to take another run at the issue. But before I could get into it, Jean waved his hand at me, and I recognized the meaning of his signal. I left the House and called Gerard Guichon, who was delighted.

Radical new approaches are always a risk in politics and government, as the Trudeau government learned when in the summer of 1969 it introduced the infamous White Paper on aboriginal policy. The document had been prepared within Jean Chrétien's Department of Indian Affairs and Northern Development. Ironically, it had been wordsmithed by Bill Fox, the writer who had helped me polish my first parliamentary speech.

Like everybody else, I had heard rumours about what would be in this discussion paper, which was intended to chart new directions for the relationship between Indians and the rest of Canadian society. For a long time, there had been talk in Indian circles about abolishing the Indian Act, about doing away with the nineteenth century paternalism that was woven through the top-down authority structure of the Indian Affairs infrastructure and devolving powers from Ottawa to Indian bands. But the talk was only talk. A few young Indian radicals were calling for the overthrow of the whole system, but calling for overthrows of complex systems was pretty standard for young radicals of all kinds in the 1960s. Among Indian elders, band leaders and the general community, there was a desire to see more powers move to the band councils to loosen some of the strings that were pulled from Ottawa. But there was no urge for revolution.

And nobody expected the Government of Canada, of all people, to offer to start one. The day before the White Paper was released, Pierre Trudeau's press secretary, Jim Davie, gave me a copy. It was a short document and didn't take long to read. Davie asked me what I thought of it. I said, "This is going to cause a lot of trouble."

The government was talking about ending the peculiar status of Indians in Canada, about abolishing the special relationship between us and the Crown that went all the way back to the King George III's Royal Proclamation of 1763. The White Paper talked about doing away with reserves, about handing the social assistance and health entitlements of Canadian Indians over to the provinces. Wewould all be equal and no different from anybody else. "A whole lotof trouble," I told the PM's PR man. The Nisga'a were the only

Indian people in the country who supported it.

I knew that the style of the Trudeau government in its early years was sometimes meant to be deliberately provocative. Pierre really believed in participatory democracy, in people getting involved from the grassroots. His idea was to get things started by putting out a White Paper that would stimulate discussion and debate, maybe even inflame feelings if that was what it took to get people up off their hind ends. The trouble was, most Canadians were not used to that kind of politics. That was why Trudeau got into trouble when he asked a crowd of Manitoba wheat farmers, "Why should I sell your wheat?" Nobody remembers that he followed up that rhetorical question with a brilliant, lucid explanation of exactly why the Government of Canada *should* be in the grain marketing business. Canadians were not used to having their governments ask them fundamental questions.

But, if Canadians in general were not used to having politicians try to stir them up and get them involved, Indians in 1969 were ten times less flexible. We had only been part of the political process for nine years. Our mature leaders had grown up in a time when it was *illegal* for Indians to hire a lawyer or raise funds to press for resolution of land claims. The country was 102 years old, and for almost all of that time nobody had given a damn what we thought about anything.

Indians were at the very bottom of a top-down power structure. All our lives, white officials had been telling us what to do. Major decisions were made at the top and trickled down through the Indian Affairs bureaucracy to the band councils: remember those pretyped resolutions the Indian Agent would bring to the meetings with the places marked for the councillors' signatures. Nothing much went the other way, except our requests for a decent level of existence. So when the Minister of Indian Affairs put out a White Paper that said Ottawa would abolish our status and throw us into the cold, unwelcoming embrace of the provinces, not many Indians said, "Oh, they're just trying to stimulate a free and spirited debate." It was not seen as a document for discussion, but as a policy that would be our undoing. Most of our leaders reacted by saying, "Like hell you will."

In retrospect, I think the White Paper did a lot of good. It shook people up, got a lot of Indians into the political process. We started to use the powers we had, and to reach for powers we didn't have but needed. Still, I would not have done it the way it was done in 1969. The White Paper created animosity and distrust that lingered for many years—among some Indians, it lingers still. Many Indians regard today's treaty process in British Columbia with suspicion left over from the White Paper. When they sit down to talk with federal negotiators, the question at the back of some minds is, "Are they still hoping to dump us into the province's lap?"

One good thing did come out of the fuss caused by the White Paper: the government began funding Indian organizations, so that we could speak for ourselves. It was an issue I had been pressing the Prime Minister on, in caucus and in occasional private conversations we had about Indian matters, ever since I became an MP. "If you want us to be part of this big debate," I would say, "then give us the resources that will let us participate fully."

But I used to add one qualifier: the government should not go on funding us forever. That would just perpetuate the sense of top-down decision-making, and put a layer of insulation between the Indian leadership and the grassroots. Now, after thirty years, I believe it is past time for the government to stop the direct funding of the Assembly of First Nations. Let most aboriginal organizations begin to pay their own way with the money flowing to the leadership from the bottom up. That's how democracy works.

The PM agreed with me and the government provided funds to allow Indian organizations to respond to the White Paper. That funding laid the basis for our people to develop a genuinely strong voice in the affairs of government that affect us. Back in the days of the North American Indian Brotherhood, old-timers such as George Manuel and I paid our own way and were proud of it, but there is no doubt that our people's cause has been better advanced since the funding of our national organizations began.

Some people, like the British Columbia constitutional gadfly Melvin Smith, disparage the efforts to put forward a national Indian voice. The consultants and lawyers who help AFN leaders and other spokespeople to prepare briefs and studies are all part of some self-perpetuating "Indian industry," they say. But don't forget that there was a long time when all the lawyers and experts were on the other side, and our leaders were helpless to prevent greedy whites from cheating us out of our land. In many parts of British Columbia, I know, the best stretches of reserve land somehow ended up in white hands—all legal and above board, according to the standards of the day—while we got the lands nobody else wanted. "We own the best rock piles in the province," was how the elders used to put it.

I was glad to be able to help reverse one of those old wrongs, by helping the Lower Nicola Band on the Shulus Reserve outside of Merritt reclaim a choice piece of ranch land, the 320-acre Tipperary Ranch, that had been carved out of the middle of the reserve. I didn't look into whatever skullduggery and sharp practice had happened decades before to turn the Shulus into a ring of poor land around its missing heart. What mattered in 1968 was that the owners of the ranch wanted to sell and had given the band first refusal.

The band was led by Chief Don Moses, then in his mid-twenties and a recent economics graduate from Simon Fraser University. Together, he and I worked on DIAND, looking for funding that the band could add to its existing financial resources and buy the ranch back. It took about seven years to complete the deal, but in the end, the band owned the Tipperary Ranch—and owned it in fee simple, so they could use it as collateral to borrow for other development projects. During all the time Don Moses and I worked on the file, no one at DIAND said anything about any policy of no more land for Indians.

My first term as a Member of Parliament lasted four years. By 1972, I was becoming an experienced practitioner of the arts of politics and governance. I knew how to get things done in Ottawa and in my riding. I was no longer an academic scientist just passing through the halls of power, no longer an outsider among the insiders.

CHAPTER 4

————

A Crack in the wall

I n 1972, Agriculture Canada reissued a 1968 publication entitled *Grassland Ranges in the Southern Interior of British Columbia*. For the reissue, the department spent a little more money than it had on the original, printing the illustrations and the cover in colour. The result was a nice looking little booklet that was immensely useful to ranchers: it told them what kind of grass grew on what ranges, in what quantities and at which seasons, so they could plan where to put their cattle. The co-authors of the pamphlet were Dr. Alastair McLean and one Leonard Marchand.

I had been the junior of the team when Alastair and I had put the data together back in the early sixties, but that little publication had been a labour of love for me. I had been happy as a research scientist with every intention of making a life's work out of studying grassland ecology. I had agreed to go to Ottawa and spend a few years as a minister's assistant because I felt I owed it to my people. Then I had fallen into politics because of the peculiar circumstances of the 1968 election, a campaign I entered not really expecting to win.

By 1972, I still pined now and then for the research lab days when I'd been perfectly content with poking around my experimental sites and writing up notes on my observations. At meetings of the Standing Committee on Agriculture, I could swap jargon with the department's bureaucrats and scientists and tell myself that I was keeping roughly current with what was happening in the research programs. But I hadn't been a working agrologist for seven years, and the re-appearance of my grasslands booklet made for a small personal milestone, reminding me that I had definitely taken a fork in the road that led away from the labs and into a life of public service.

I didn't fall into the campaign of 1972; I chose to stand for re-election, because I felt I was being useful to my constituents and my people. I don't know if I was fated to be in public life, but in 1972 I was again a willing horse. If the voters wanted me back, I would do my best for them.

One last word on the grasslands booklet: it didn't hurt my credibility to have my name on this authoritative publication that could be found in just about every rancher's home. And in the election of that year, I needed every scrap of help I could lay hands on.

I certainly wasn't getting much from Pierre Trudeau. The Prime Minister was giving Canadians a taste of philosopher-kingship. He was out delivering speeches so dull that they could have doubled as academic lectures. He had decided to run on the government's record and to set out in dispassionate terms—he called it "a conversation with Canadians"—the ideas and goals the Liberals would pursue if we were returned to office. A true democrat, he thought that politics ought to be about appealing to people's heads and forgot that many are frequently more ruled by the heart. He had set aside the experienced party election apparatus, personified by Senator Keith Davey, and turned the campaign over to a group of idealistic amateurs who thought that all that was needed were some feel-good commercials and a slogan—"The Land Is Strong"—that set a new standard for empty blather.

We rank-and-file candidates, searching for votes on the public's doorsteps, kept waiting for the boss to catch fire the way he had in 1968. The Liberal record was good. The economy was performing well. In October, 1970, the government had weathered the worst crisis of civil disorder since the 1919 Winnipeg General Strike, taking resolute action against terrorists and murderers in a manner that had won the support of 87 per cent of Canadians—the highest approval rating of any government in our country's history.

Yet now we were struggling to keep our noses above water. A big part of the problem in Kamloops-Cariboo was the know-nothing reaction to the Official Languages Act (OLA). I couldn't count the number of times I was told by angry constituents that Ottawa was "trying to shove French down our throats," as if people expected to be rounded up and force-fed the country's other official language. I never did see how putting the word "Sortie" next to the "Exit" sign at a federal airport amounted to a threat to any British Columbian's right to speak English. But I could definitely see how it wasn't right that French Canadians were paying taxes to support a government that couldn't speak to them in their own language, when their ancestors had been here for four hundred years. Granted, it's not as long as my people have been here, but it's still a respectable chunk of time, and ought to count for something.

The OLA was one of the emotional issues that were a big part of the 1972 election out on the doorsteps. My campaign team, again headed by Jarl Whist, kept hoping that Pierre Trudeau would somehow rekindle the magic of 1968. But it may be that the boss himself had never really been all that exciting back during the Trudeaumania hoopla; maybe it was just that we Canadians wanted to be excited about something, and we'd hung our feelings on him to the point where we couldn't see—and maybe didn't care—what was underneath. But, when he came to Kamloops, he still drew three or four thousand people; they still wanted to be seen with him, to be photographed with him, to touch him. Whether it came from him or came from them, there was still something *there*, and when he changed tack in the final weeks of the campaign, it gave us a narrow victory instead of a thorough defeat.

Just before the election was called, Trudeau had thrown another anchor to the Liberal candidates treading water in BC, when he had expressed his view at a meeting in Vancouver that there was "no such thing as aboriginal title in British Columbia." Added to the outrage stirred up by the 1969 White Paper on Indians that was still boiling among my people, his statement on the land claims issue had dealt a solid blow to the chances of Liberals running in ridings that had any sizeable Indian population.

It didn't do a whole lot for my personal morale, either. I was there when he said it. I went home to my riding, thinking "What the hell am I doing this for? Why not just give up and go back to research?"

If a man as learned and liberal as Pierre Trudeau doesn't see the justice of our cause, what hope do we have? But the moment of despair passed. I thought of all the work by Andy Paull, and George Manuel, and Frank Calder and James Gosnell of the Nisga'a, and so many others. I knew they would keep fighting, and so would I, just as our elders had done; when you come right down to it, what else could we do?

Intellectually, I knew that the "no such thing" quote was an instance of Trudeau's playing the academic law professor, taking the purely legalistic view based on what the courts had been saying up until that time. I knew that he was one of the most sincere defenders of people's rights who had ever sat in the prime minister's chair at the cabinet table. But when I heard him say those words, it hurt. There again was the blank wall that we Indians in British Columbia had been throwing ourselves against for generations.

I was saddened but not surprised when Forrie Walkem, Chief of the Cook's Ferry Band at Spence's Bridge and an officer of the Union of BC Indian Chiefs, reacted to the PM's remark by urging all Indians in BC not to vote Liberal. Fortunately, there were other voices to speak up on my behalf: Chief Harvey Jules of the Adam's Lake Band and Chief Hy Eustache of the North Thompson Band urged my Indian constituents to vote for me. And the polls later showed that my people had continued to give me their trust. If they hadn't, these would be the recollections of a man who had spent his life studying grass.

On October 30, with Jarl Whist holding his breath as the Salmon Arm polls reported in, I was first past the post by a squeaky narrow margin of 736 votes which was reduced to 714 in the official final count. I had been helped by my performance as a good constituency MP—personally answering every piece of mail and fighting doggedly to defeat the Shuswap diversion project had surely made a difference. The Tory candidate was a doctor from Merritt named Roy Hewson, who added a mean-spirited tone to the campaign when he made a fuss about some paper Indian head-dresses worn by some of the kids around the campaign when they went out to welcome Trudeau the day he came to visit. "If I had wanted to use my people, we'd wear cowboy hats and boots," the Conservative candidate sneered, turning a harmless teenage lark into a means of dividing the community. That old chestnut—if you can't say something nice, don't say anything—is not a bad guildline in politics.

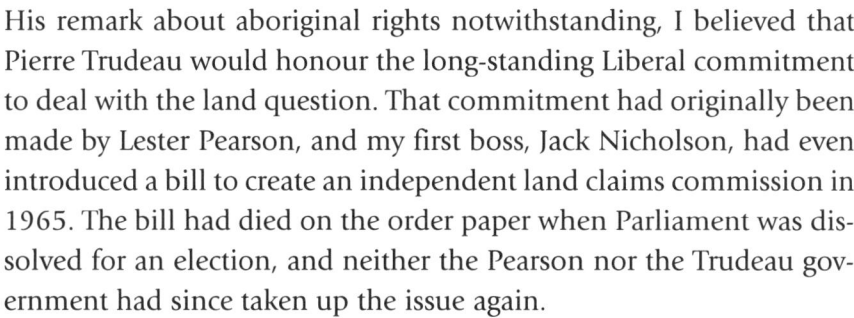

His remark about aboriginal rights notwithstanding, I believed that Pierre Trudeau would honour the long-standing Liberal commitment to deal with the land question. That commitment had originally been made by Lester Pearson, and my first boss, Jack Nicholson, had even introduced a bill to create an independent land claims commission in 1965. The bill had died on the order paper when Parliament was dissolved for an election, and neither the Pearson nor the Trudeau government had since taken up the issue again.

There was little likelihood in 1972 that any action on Indian matters would be forthcoming. For one thing, our minority government was mainly focused on day to day survival tactics. Besides, the Indian reaction to the White Paper had convinced Trudeau that our people were not looking to Ottawa for drastic changes, and he had made it clear that he would do nothing about amending the Indian Act or other big issues until we in the Indian community had formulated our own positions and brought them to the discussion table. To use the expression of the day, the ball was in our people's court, and he would await direction from the grassroots and through the Indian leadership before doing anything.

Trudeau remained concerned about Indian affairs, however, and we had frequent conversations about the issues. I continued to lobby in caucus—where any MP can speak bluntly to ministers and the PM-so that our concerns were kept on the stove, if not on the front burner. I had two main themes: first, that the three things our people needed most were education, education and education; second, that the Government of Canada should provide the funds to allow our people to go to the courts and there seek a resolution of the land question in British Columbia. The Prime Minister was entitled to believe that there was no such thing as aboriginal title, but we'd like to know what the Supreme Court of Canada had to say on the matter.

The government agreed, and underwrote the costs of a case that had worked its way up through the BC Court of Appeal to the

highest court of our country. It was brought by the Nisga'a, who were
suing the Crown of British Columbia to gain a legal determination of
the status of the land they had occupied in northwestern BC since
time immemorial. Like almost all Indian peoples in British
Columbia, they had signed no treaties and had never been conquered, and therefore they maintained that they still held aboriginal
title to the Nass Valley. The case was heard in the name of one of the
hereditary chiefs of the Nisga'a, Frank Calder, who had signed the
court documents for his people. The principals in the Calder case
would often use my Parliament Hill office as a place to meet and plan
their strategy in the fall of 1972. Fortunately, by then, a series of
reforms had changed the House of Commons rules, and each MP was
now allowed two small rooms; otherwise, we would have been
jammed together like sardines.

On January 31, 1973, they were all gathered in my offices at
Rooms 131S and 133S in the Centre Block: Frank Calder, Bill McKay,
James Gosnell (whose younger brother, Joe Gosnell would one day
sign the Nisga'a Treaty), Tony and Rod Robinson, George Manuel and
Senator Guy Williams. At about ten in the morning, the seven
Supreme Court Justices delivered their judgment, and it was a
groundbreaker.

The Justices had brought down a decision that was split three
ways. One had dismissed the case on the technical grounds that, in
those days, no one could sue the Crown in British Columbia without
first obtaining the Crown's consent to be sued—a fiat was the legal
term—and since the Government of British Columbia had not given
that permission, the case could not be heard. The other six Justices
had overlooked that technicality and had addressed the case on its
merits. Three ruled that the Nisga'a had indeed once had aboriginal
title to the Nass Valley, but that it had been extinguished when BC
joined Confederation. The remaining three members of the Supreme
Court of Canada gave as their opinion that the Nisga'a had not only
had aboriginal title before 1871, but that *they had it still*.

It was a great breakthrough. The highest court in the land had not
resolved the issue of aboriginal title, but the Justices had made it clear
that there was an issue to be decided. The delegation read the judg-

ment in my office and immediately came to a decision: we must have a reaction from the Government of Canada, and it must come from the Prime Minister. I called Indian Affairs and Northern Development Minister Jean Chrétien at home—he was away from the office with a medical problem—and he agreed: the PM should meet with the Indians.

It was just going on 2:15, the start of the daily Question Period, and I knew that Trudeau would be heading down to the House. As I was by then the Parliamentary Secretary (PS) to the ailing Minister, I had to be there myself to answer any questions that would have otherwise been directed to Jean Chrétien. I went up to the Chamber, which was almost directly above my offices, and tried to get through the swirl of people who usually surrounded the PM's desk just before the afternoon sitting resumed—it was a good time to try to get his attention on one issue or another. I told him I had the Calder case delegation in my office and that I thought he should meet with them. I don't think he heard me over the noise—at least, I got no response—and now the Speaker was calling the House to order, so I took my seat.

It soon became clear that, although the Supreme Court decision was one topic of that day's Question Period, it was too big an issue to throw at the lowly PS to an ailing minister. Frank Howard, the NDP critic for Indian Affairs, and John Diefenbaker, who appointed himself the Conservative critic on any issue he took an interest in, aimed their shots directly at Trudeau. How would the Prime Minister respond to this Supreme Court judgment? The Prime Minister said coolly that he would have to read it first.

I went back to my office and told the anxious delegation that we weren't in the door yet, but I would keep trying. Then I went back up to the Chamber. My seat, now that I was a PS, was closer to those of the big guns and within hailing distance of the Prime Minister. Again, I asked the PM to meet with the people waiting in my office. This time he replied, but only to say he could not meet with them before he had read the judgment, but at least I knew that he now had it before him.

I went back down again to my offices and reported the news. They urged me to try again, so I went upstairs a third time into the

Chamber and right to the PM's desk. I won't say I shouted or made a fuss, but I spoke as forcefully as I ever have in my life, forcefully enough that I worried that I was about to anger the most powerful man in the country—who also happened to be my boss.

I said, "Pierre, you just *have* to see these guys. This is the most important case that has ever been judged in the Supreme Court on aboriginal title and the land question in BC, and all the important leaders are in my office waiting to come and hear what you have to say."

He frowned a little and told me to wait. I went to my seat, behind and a little off to his right, and I waited, not too patiently. He was reading the judgment. At ten to three, he looked over his shoulder and beckoned me. "Bring them to my office after Question Period," he said.

I went back down and we waited, listening to the end of Question Period on the little squawk-box that piped the sound feed from the Chamber into every MP's office. When the House moved on to the afternoon's business, I led the delegation up to meet the Prime Minister. Trudeau welcomed us into his private office, shaking hands with each of the Indian leaders and congratulating them on the judgment. There weren't enough chairs, so I stood at the back of the room, as Frank Calder stated the Nisga'a position. He wasn't as blunt as Chief James Gosnell had been a few months earlier, when he'd said that "We own BC—lock, stock and barrel," but he was direct and told the PM that they had been cheated out of their land, that now three Justices of the Supreme Court had validated the Nisga'a claim to aboriginal title, and that they wanted a land settlement. Some of the other chiefs added their comments. The upshot of it was that the ball was now back on the government's side of the net.

The Prime Minister heard them out. He asked a few questions on minor details of the case, then said he wanted to think about what the government ought to do. He would not give a commitment at that moment. But then he led all of us out into the corridor, where the reporters and camera crews were waiting for the post-Question Period scrum. And there he said to the Nisga'a, with the media's tape recorders running, "I guess you guys have more rights than I thought you did."

It sounded like a casual observation, but I believe it was a calculated signal as to which way the government was going to move. For me, those few breezy words took away the lingering sting of his "no such thing as aboriginal title" remark. More important, I could look again at that blank wall against which our people had been hurling ourselves for a century in British Columbia, and for the first time, I could see a crack.

I had been made Parliamentary Secretary to the Minister of Indian Affairs and Northern Development soon after I returned to Ottawa in the fall of 1972. There was no grand ceremony involved: Trudeau phoned to ask me if I wanted to be PS to Jean Chrétien, I said, "Sure," and that was it. For some MPs, the position is almost a sinecure, especially for those who are appointed, for reasons of geographic or even ethnic balance, to assist ministers who don't particularly want their help. But I was a very active PS. I knew every file on the department's agenda, and you might say I had been involved with Indian Affairs in one way or another since November 16, 1933.

Since Jean Chrétien was afflicted with a chronic, but not too serious, health problem in those days, I took on more of the ministerial load than most PSs do, taking Question Period for him several times. I was confident in the House now, a veteran who had come a long way since the day in September, 1968 when I had seconded the motion to accept the Speech From the Throne. The days when I half expected to hear someone say, "Hey, Indian, what are you doing here?" had long since faded. I rarely had to call up my father's words to steady me; I enjoyed crossing swords with the opposition critics from time to time, although in Chrétien's absence I would usually just take questions on notice to be replied to later in writing.

Sometimes, however, the duty was less enjoyable, as in the time I filled in for the Minister as guest—and punching bag—in a free-for-all CTV interview program called *Under Attack* that was being filmed at Carleton University. Donna and I went, and it was mean. The program lived up—or down—to its name, inviting the audience to take shots at the interviewee, and on this occasion the audience was mainly radical young Indians and their non-Indian groupies.

Some of the radicals had always had a particular dislike for me, calling me "apple" and "Uncle Tomahawk," so the questioning was mainly in the spirit of "Have you stopped beating your wife yet?" After a while, I gave up trying to unload the loaded questions and give straight answers to the people in the auditorium. Instead, since I had no hope of convincing anyone in the bleachers—they had come to attack, not to discuss—I turned to the cameras and spoke directly to the people who were watching somewhere out in televisionland.

But, much as I have always rejected the tactics of radicalism, which often seem to me to be more about making the protesters feel superior than about actually achieving any concrete results, there have been many times when I have been torn. I remember the opening of Parliament after the 1972 election, when a group of militants who had set up a native people's "embassy" on an island in the Ottawa river came up to the Hill en masse to protest. It was a cold, wet, miserable day, and the radicals were outside the doors of the Peace Tower, some beating on a drum and chanting while others shouted slogans. There had been loose talk that they might try to disrupt the opening ceremonies, and the Commons security officials had called out the RCMP riot squad.

The Mounties came in formation, with shields and helmets and batons, and put themselves between the protesters and the big doors that had been chained shut. Their appearance set the militants off into even louder drumming and slogan shouting. I watched from a window that overlooked the confrontation, and I felt frankly lousy. The radicals were wrong in their tactics, and their motivations may sometimes have leaned toward self-aggrandizement. But they were right on the issues. I was with them on the issues. The situation of our people in Canada was not good. In many places, it was a disgrace.

Sometimes I would ask myself, "How can it be like this? Why are we treated this way?" I had thanked John Diefenbaker for giving us the vote, but the questions I had never put to my colleagues in the Liberal Party were, "Why did we have to wait for Diefenbaker's government to act? Where was the Liberal Party when we needed them?" I remembered how a great Liberal like Jack Pickersgill, who had been the minister responsible for Indian Affairs under Louis St. Laurent, had stood up during the debate over the voting rights bill and praised Ellen Fairclough, the Tory minister who carried the ball for Dief's government. But if he was so much in favour of Indian suffrage, why hadn't he brought in a bill to give Indians the vote when he was in office? Was it because the current of racism that ran through Canadian society was so deep that it cowed even the Cabinet? Or was it just that we were Canada's forgotten people, a bunch of nobodies, who had to wait for a Prime Minister who—for all Diefenbaker's faults—was not afraid to do what was right, and damn the consequences?

These were the kinds of questions I deliberately put aside during my political career. Digging into the past to trace the blame stirred up the bitter dregs down in the bottom of the heart, and that was a drain on the spirit for no particular gain. I have always believed that you won your rounds by using your head, not your heart. And I think my career has been a testament to the wisdom of doing what can be done today and leaving the past where it lies.

There is, admittedly, some satisfaction in pointing the finger and calling down the judgment of history on those who hurt us or who stood by and did not help us when we were in need. But it's pretty thin soup compared to the knowledge that you've actually solved a problem and made life better in some way for real people, here and now. Radicalism did not get us the vote or an education or a place at the tables where big decisions are made. It never will get us anything because the numbers will always be against us. We will never be more than a tiny fraction of the population of Canada. If we "fight the power" using methods outside the rules of civilized democracy, we will always be defeated. As my old friend Chief Gordon Antoine of the Coldwater Band used to say, the reason we were herded onto reserves and lost our land was because "the white guys always had more guns than we did." They still do.

The young militants of today, Indian and non-Indian, were not born when our country was last faced with an attempt by radicals to overthrow the political process. But those of us who were in public life when terrorists of the Front de Liberation du Québec kidnapped British trade commissioner James Cross, then seized and murdered

Québec's Minister of Labour, Pierre Laporte, will not forget the helpless rage we felt against those who were out to steal our democratic rights and replace them with a power that came only from the barrels of their guns.

I was within earshot of Pierre Trudeau when a reporter asked him on the steps of Parliament how far he would go to combat terrorism, and he answered, "Just watch me." In caucus he had told us that he considered the War Measures Act "a very blunt instrument that I don't enjoy using." He was plainly upset about what was happening in his home province, but he was resolute in his determination to protect the rule of law. I supported him utterly.

I was in the House on the evening of Saturday, October 17, during the emergency debate on the imposition of the War Measures Act, sitting next to the MP from Prince George, Bob Borrie, who was speaking on the motion. A page brought a note for him, but didn't want to interrupt while he was speaking. I took it, and handed it to Bob when he paused. He opened it, read it, then informed the House that Pierre Laporte's body had been found in the trunk of a car at a Québec airport.

I went to Pierre Laporte's funeral, although Donna didn't want me to go. I had never met the man, but I believed his death was a challenge to every Canadian who gave a damn about our democracy. I was sickened and filled with anger against those FLQ thugs. My people had fought so hard for the right to vote, the right to participate with dignity in the democratic process. Now these criminals were trying to wipe it all away with the wave of a pistol. How dare they set themselves above the rights of the people?

When we Indians won the federal vote, it was through dignified lobbying by our national leaders. That, and the justice of our cause, were what moved Dief to give us the status of full citizens in our own land. It was the single most important piece of legislation that has affected our people in my lifetime, and it came from a proper use of the political system. My message to young Indians is: get involved. Politics is not quick and easy, and sometimes you have to push for years to get the door to open. But it's how you make things really change.

There was more to being a parliamentary secretary than arguing with radicals and filling in for Jean Chrétien. One afternoon in the House, Trudeau called me over to his desk after Question Period. He had recently returned from a visit to New Zealand, where he had been impressed by the way the Maoris had come to participate in the life of the country. He said, "Why don't you get a group together and go down there, see if you can learn anything that might work for Canada?"

I had never planned a foreign trip, so I talked to Jean Chrétien and some of the departmental officials and set about organizing a delegation to go to New Zealand. Since we would be in the neighbourhood, we thought it might also be instructive to visit Australia and see how things stood with the aborigines. I assembled a non-partisan group consisting of Frank Howard, the Skeena MP who was the NDP's Indian Affairs critic, Erik Nielsen, the Yukon MP and Tory critic, Bud Orange, the Liberal MP from the NWT and Ian Watson, a Liberal who represented a Montreal riding and chaired the Indian Affairs committee. We also asked George Manuel to join us, as well as Bill Mussell, a member of the Skwah Band near Chilliwack who was a special assistant to Jean Chrétien. The Canadian Forces had recently taken delivery of a new Boeing 707 and were conducting long-distance training and familiarization flights. So we were able to use the plane for our whole trip, across the Pacific to New Zealand, then on to Australia.

We had an official tour of some Maori settlements, and met some of their leaders as well as the white man who was the minister in charge of Maori affairs in the New Zealand government. It was interesting and at times instructive—the Maori had really integrated themselves into the country's society and institutions, far more than our people had in Canada—but I soon realized that I had made a mistake in letting our officials and the New Zealanders put together the itinerary. It wasn't as if we were being shown a lot of "Potemkin villages," those cheerfully sanitized facades the Soviets would set up to gull visitors who wanted to see communism in all its glory, but we were not seeing the full picture. George Manuel went off by himself to meet some ordinary Maoris, and came back with a less rosy view, but the rest of us were trapped in a series of formal meetings and polite cocktail receptions. It was a mistake I wouldn't make again.

We then flew over to Australia to be chauffeured around on more officially sanctioned outings, but not even the full weight of diplomatic niceties could disguise how truly horrible was the plight of the aborigines. The living conditions of the people were heartbreaking: "Like Indian Affairs thirty years ago," was how George Manuel described it, everything controlled from the top down and smothered under an appalling blanket of white-man-knows-best paternalism. The aborigines living under this system were without a doubt the most depressed people I have ever seen.

The only cheerful note came at a little community a few miles outside Darwin in Australia's tropical north. The officials had turned out the whole community to meet us—maybe a couple of hundred people, most of them children or teenagers. We were introduced as visitors from Canada, and I'm willing to bet that most of the folks there didn't know what Canada was or where it was or why we might have come to see them. The aborigines looked at us looking at them, and it was clear they weren't impressed, not even when one of the Australian officials told them that three of us were "Red Indians."

We stood there feeling increasingly dumb, until George Manuel saved the day by reaching into his duffel bag and pulling out a full size, eagle feather headdress, the kind that were originally worn only by the Sioux, but which Hollywood had made a universal symbol of the North American Indian. George put on his feathers, then he brought a drum out of the bag and began to beat it, while moving into the steps of a friendship dance. The aborigine kids had seen American westerns at the movie theatres in Darwin; they started whooping that "woo-woo-woo" call that movie Indians used to make, popping their open hands against their mouths. Bill Mussell and I joined in, and we taught the aborigines a simple friendship dance. For a few minutes, we managed to break free of the diplomatic box the official power structure had built to contain us.

I was perhaps more effective as a member of the Indian Affairs committee. Standing committees had much more scope for action in the Trudeau years, and we put forward a number of measures to dismantle the old paternalism and give Indians more power over their own lives. One small example: when I was in university, all my fees and living expense were paid for me by the department; not a penny passed through my hands. It didn't bother me—all I cared about was getting an education—but it was part of the father-knows-best attitude the department showed toward us. But while I was on the Indian Affairs committee, we put together a research paper on Indian control of Indian education, which helped change a lot of the department's policy. Young Indian adults were eventually given the funds for their education directly to spend themselves. And the system worked fine.

Politics is a strain on family life, and in my day the House of Commons sat long into the evening. Being a parliamentary secretary brought more money and a staff assistant seconded from the department, but it also meant more work and less time that I could spend with my family. I tried to be an attentive husband and father, to have breakfast with the kids every day when I was home. And we made it a practice, when I was in Ottawa, to have dinner together every Friday night in the Parliamentary restaurant. The kids would always make a fuss over Jean Marchand if he happened to come in: they had decided he was some kind of cousin, and they would run over to his table—at the risk of upsetting a waiter or two—to see him. Oddly enough, when the researcher Jean-Jacques Séguin traced my Québec roots, it turned out that Jean Marchand was indeed some kind of distant relation.

But sharing breakfasts and dinners are no substitute for the kind of family life I had known when I was a child at Six Mile Creek. We were a farm family, all working together and living together. As the only boy in the house, in an era when gender differences were taken for granted, I spent almost all of my growing-up time with my dad, riding together and working in the hayfields. I couldn't do anything like that with my son and daughter, and I felt guilty for it. I would have liked to have had more time to go fishing with them or to

Family photo for our 1978 Christmas card. Len Jr. was nursing a broken thumb, obtained while playing quarterback for the Gloucester Giants.

wander around in the hills back home, teaching them the Okanagan names of things, the way my father had taught me. But though we spent the summers back in the riding, and I taught them how to ride, I wish there could have been more.

As a boy and a young man, I always enjoyed going to the rodeos. I knew many of the cowboys—some of them were my cousins—and I loved every minute spent on the rodeo grounds. After I entered politics, hitting the rodeo circuit in my riding became one of the best parts of the job. I could visit with constituents to keep in touch with how people felt about the issues of the day, and at the same time watch the bronc riders and calf ropers. Often, someone would lend me a horse and I would ride in the opening parade.

When they were old enough, I would usually take my kids with me, and I guess it never occurred to me that they might not enjoy the events as much as I did—until one very hot and dusty July day when we were at a rodeo on the Deadman's Creek Reserve. I was in my element, talking horses and politics, when I felt a tug on my shirt. I glanced down and there was Len Jr., maybe nine or ten years old, looking pretty fed up. "Dad," he said, "if we have to go to one more rodeo, I'm quitting politics!"

Donna was the glue that held us all together. She took on the task of being the wife of a full-time politician and a part-time husband and father, and did a first-rate job of it. The credit for our still being together after almost four decades goes mainly to her.

I did make sure that the kids learned to swim. I never really have mastered swimming, so my role in teaching the kids to swim was mostly that of a bad example: I had to stay on shore while the Prime Minister swam with Lori and Len at the family parties he threw at his summer residence on Harrington Lake. Pierre was very good with kids—mine, other people's and his own. Lori and Len liked him, and he always remembered their names.

After the January 31 meeting between Trudeau and the Calder case delegation, I was anxious to get a response from the Prime Minister on what would happen next, and I nudged him and Jean Chrétien whenever I had an opportunity. But we were a minority in the House, and all of us on our side of the aisle were conscious that the Opposition could shut everything down and throw us into an election any time there was a vote. So the minds of the PM and Cabinet tended to be concentrated, wonderfully or not, on getting through each day's sitting without Trudeau's having to visit the Governor-General. Instead of breaking for the summer return to the ridings in June, we went right through July, with the NDP using their balance-of-power position to encourage us to do a number of things—create PetroCan and the Foreign Investment Review Agency, for example—which most of the caucus wanted to do anyway.

That summer, I saw a first-hand instance of how Trudeau had been right when he had snapped at some opposition members that they were "just nobodies" once they were fifty yards from Parliament Hill. On one of those hot, muggy Ottawa evenings, I went out for an after work beer with Doug Stewart and a few other MPs. Walking along the Sparks Street Mall, we were maybe three or four hundred yards from the Commons Chamber, where the high-stress political opera that surrounds a minority government was the moment-by-moment preoccupation of every MP. But not one of us backbenchers was recognized. We might just as well have been another handful of Ottawa civil servants threading our way through the tourists. And when Doug tried an informal sampling of the public's political awareness by asking randomly chose passersby what was happening in Parliament, most people didn't know, and didn't much care.

In August, after the House finally rose and as I was preparing to join Donna and the kids out in the riding, an invitation came to have lunch with Pierre Trudeau and Jean Chrétien at 24 Sussex Drive. The topic was to be how the government would respond to Indian land claims in BC in light of the Calder decision. We ate at the end of an elegant table that would have seated twenty, Trudeau at the head and Jean and I to either side. There was some small talk that I don't recall, and the food was probably excellent, though I don't remember that either: I was too excited about the business we were there for.

Lunch over, Jean Chrétien made a brief pitch, with me chiming in. We reminded the PM of the commitment the Pearson government had made to create an independent land claims commission before the 1965 election. When he had become Minister of Justice in 1967, Trudeau had questioned the validity of that commitment, part of the thinking that later led him to say that there was "no such thing as aboriginal title in British Columbia."

The Prime Minister was still not warm toward the idea of an independent commission, operating at arm's length from government. If BC Indians had rights, and the Supreme Court seemed to be saying they did, then he believed that the responsibility for dealing with them belonged in the hands of the people's elected representatives, not some bloodless appointed body. This was a political matter, to be dealt with by Cabinet, through the Minister of Indian Affairs and Northern Development. Jean Chrétien was to find a way for the

Government of Canada to conduct land claims negotiations with the Nisga'a.

Jean and I drove back to Parliament Hill, but if the car had broken down I could easily have flown. Back at my desk, I phoned George Manuel at the National Indian Brotherhood office in Ottawa and told him to keep it under his hat until the official announcement, but everything our people had worked for since the days of Andy Paull was now within reach. I phoned my old friend Gus Gottfriedsen in the riding. I was grinning like the disappearing cat in the Disney cartoon. I had to put down an urge to yell like a bronc-buster at the Ashcroft rodeo—you don't do that kind of thing in Parliament.

Then I leaned back and looked out through the windows at a beautiful, sunny afternoon, and I let it all sink in. This was the most momentous day of my career as a politician to that time. I had played a part in bringing about a crucial change in the policy of the Government of Canada. I hadn't beaten any drums or chained myself to any public buildings. Instead, I had been a constant, quiet voice at the centre of power, and I had helped redirect that power onto a path that would at last bring my people justice. Nobody was going to hand me a medal or name a mountain after me for being a good lobbyist—the credit for the policy would go to the minister and the government in general—but I knew what my role had been, and I was satisfied.

As I write this, it is twenty-six years later. The Nisga'a Treaty has been signed by the Government of British Columbia and ratified by the Legislative Assembly. It now awaits ratification by the Parliament of Canada. There have been many bends and twists in the trail since that lunch at 24 Sussex Drive, but there is one thing that I believed then that I believe just as strongly today: it is essential that the aboriginal people of Canada—Indians, Inuit and Métis—be part of the common political apparatus of our country. We must sit at the tables where the decisions that shape our lives are made. And the only way to win a seat at those tables is to run and be elected to public office.

I am proud to have been the first of my kind to sit in the House of Commons. I am proud of what I did there. Because I don't believe in dwelling on the past, I don't lament the fact that it took 101 years for one of us to hold the office of Canadian Member of Parliament. But it worries me that, thirty-one years after I was first elected, I am not only the first, but still the *only*, Indian from BC to make it into government. There must be more of us. More of our young people— our young professionals—must join political parties, go for nominations, run for office, and *win*.

To use the old phrase, that is where the action is. Politics is where things get done.

The Government of Canada had committed itself to negotiate with the Nisga'a; that meant that two out of three of the parties to any land claims negotiation were ready to sit down and talk. Jean Chrétien made arrangements to meet with the third player, and we flew out to see Norm Levi, the minister responsible for Indians, and specifically for the Nisga'a file, in the Government of British Columbia.

The position of successive BC governments on the land claims issue had always been the same: the problem had been settled generations before when the Province had set aside reserve lands for Indians, which became the responsibility of the Dominion government after BC joined Confederation in 1871. Indians themselves were entirely a federal matter, as far as BC was concerned, and therefore there was no reason why British Columbia should enter into any talks about land claims.

Of course, the rub was that the Crown of British Columbia, under the terms of the British North America Act, held virtually all public land in the province, including all the territory that our people claimed we had been cheated out of when those postage-stamp parcels of poor land were being doled out to us as our only birthright. The Province's position put us into a classic Catch-22 situation: we could talk land claims, but only with the level of government that held none of the land, while the government that did hold our land wouldn't talk to us at all.

We had hopes that the Catch 22 would dissolve now that Dave Barrett's NDP government was sitting around the cabinet table in Victoria. The federal NDP, particularly their Indian Affairs critic Frank

Howard, the MP whose riding of Skeena on the northern BC coast included the Nisga'a territory, were gung-ho for land claims talks. Howard had been hammering away at Chrétien and Trudeau ever since the Calder decision.

Mr. Levi was a mild and pleasant man. He received us cordially. There were many pleasantries batted back and forth. But when we tried to get a firm response on the substance of what we had come to talk about, the NDP minister slid gracefully away. I had been around politicians long enough to recognize the old soft shoe. Barrett's NDP, for all their posturing and rhetoric, were no different from the W.A.C. Bennett's Socreds on the question of land claims. We were, oh-so-politely, shut out.

CHAPTER 5

"No oil port. No way."

C ompared to 1972, the election campaign of 1974 was a piece of cake. Things couldn't have gone better. Merv Chertkow, a Kamloops lawyer and a longtime friend, was campaign chair, and everything ran like clockwork. The closest thing to a hitch in an otherwise unbroken string of happy days was when Finance Minister John Turner visited the riding. He was to be the featured speaker at the campaign's big luncheon and rally in Quesnel, and a plane had been chartered to pick all of us up in Kamloops and fly us to the north end of the riding; we were on a tight schedule, with the flight timed to put us in the hall just in time for lunch and Turner's speech.

We all rode out to the Kamloops airport, but the plane wasn't there. It turned out that the pilot had got his instructions backwards—he had flown to Quesnel, expecting to collect us for a flight to Kamloops. There were no planes immediately ready for hire, and we were feeling pretty stuck until John Turner looked out the terminal windows and saw a private jet just touching down on the runway. He had his aide ask the radio operator in the tower to call the jet and find out who owned it, and word came back that it belonged to the Ranger Oil Company, whose president and chief executive officer, John M. (Jack) Pierce, was on board.

Turner knew the man well, so he got on the radio phone and said, "Jack, we're in a jam. Can you give us a flip up to Quesnel?" For half an hour of private conversation with the Minister of Finance, the CEO was more than willing to burn a little corporate jet fuel. We took off within minutes, and managed to get Turner up to the speaker's podium in Quesnel just as the crowd was finishing lunch. As he launched into his speech, I could see our local campaign crew, Lance Lea, Lon Godfrey and Gloria Lazzarin, wiping the sweat from their brows.

This was my third election, and the days of "Who, me?" were long behind me. I didn't consider myself a "professional" politician, as Ron Basford used to describe himself. I still thought of myself as a guy who was doing a job, although now it was a job I knew how to do. I was comfortable on the doorsteps, no different from the people who opened their doors to talk to me. I'd had a campaign button back during the 1968 campaign that said "Politics is People"—I believed that was true, and that I was one of the people.

It didn't hurt that I was well received everywhere I went that summer. I remember door-knocking through four blocks in the Kamloops suburb of Westsyde one day, and getting the vote of virtually every person I spoke with. People knew that I had worked hard for the constituency, and the fuss about the Official Languages Act and "French shoved down our throats" had pretty well died down. The voters liked Trudeau again, liked his vision of where we ought to be going.

They didn't care for the way the NDP had used their balance of power position to drive their agenda in Ottawa, and in BC the Barrett government's fumblings had taken so much of the shine off the social democrats that labour leader Paddy Neale actually lost the NDP stronghold of Vancouver East to Art Lee, a rookie Liberal candidate who was also the second person of Chinese ancestry to sit in the Commons. The NDP candidate in Kamloops-Cariboo, Ron Anderson, was so short of workers he had to drive himself to campaign events, which can be dangerous when the fatigue of being constantly on the go for several weeks catches up with you. One night, he apparently fell asleep at the wheel and drove into Nicola Lake; thank goodness he survived, but the car was never recovered.

Bob Stanfield had not caught fire with the electorate in my riding. I was also helped by the fact that my Conservative opponent, Don Couch, was a recent arrival from New Zealand who was not even a Canadian citizen. The NDP were not then a serious factor in federal campaigns in the area, but the Social Credit Party of Canada ran a candidate who must have taken some votes from the Tory. I had been so confident about winning that Donna and I had bought our first house in Ottawa—a little place in the east end of town—three months before the election. While we'd been away campaigning, our friends and Bayshore neighbours Gene and Frances Lotochinski had moved everything in for us. I came back to Parliament amid a certain amount of speculation that I would be appointed to the Cabinet, since BC had lost a cabinet minister with Fisheries Minister Jack Davis's defeat in North Vancouver and I was second only to Ron Basford in seniority among BC MPs.

In the midst of that speculation, I found myself faced with the need to make a moral choice. Ron Basford had been Minister of Urban Affairs in the pre-election cabinet, but the word was going around that he was to be reassigned to the National Revenue portfolio, which was usually given to a rookie minister. Ron felt, with justification, that he did not deserve a demotion, having just led the campaign that had doubled the number of Liberal MPs from our province; he was telling friends that, if he was offered National Revenue, he would resign. I decided that I could not accept a portfolio if the senior MP from British Columbia was to leave the cabinet under such circumstances. It was a matter of loyalty. I went to Ron and told him as much, and let it be known in the appropriate circles that I would refuse the call if it came.

As it happened, Ron was persuaded to accept Revenue, and acquitted himself so well in that post that within less than a year he was promoted to Minister of Justice and Attorney General for Canada. I was not offered a cabinet position that year: the Prime Minister instead asked Senator Ray Perrault to be Leader of the Government in the Senate, a post which automatically brings a seat in Cabinet. In the smaller cabinets of those times, two spots were all that British Columbia could expect. I didn't much mind being passed over for Ray: he was a good friend and, as a former MP and Liberal leader in the provincial legislature, he brought a lot of experience to the job.

Then came a call from Pierre, asking me if I wanted to serve another stint as a parliamentary secretary, this time to two ministers—Jeanne Sauvé and Romeo LeBlanc—who shared the dual

portfolios of Ministers of Environment and Fisheries. The big department had been put together for Jack Davis, but now the intent was to
separate the two jurisdictions, although I think nobody realized how
long and complex a process that separation would entail.

I got along well with Jeanne Sauvé, who was a new MP, although
not new to Parliament: her husband Maurice had been a major
Québec Liberal on the Hill before the Trudeau years. Because I had
served on the Standing Committee on Energy, Mines and Resources,
which oversaw environmental affairs, I was up to date on all the files
affecting her side of the department. In caucus, my scientific training
had put me in a position to advise the Prime Minister and previous
ministers on environmental issues. So, all in all, I was just the kind of
PS a rookie minister needed.

And Jeanne Sauvé was just the kind of minister I needed at that
time. She gave me plenty of scope to use my abilities and experience.
I took Question Period for her a number of times, and I played a
major role in shepherding the first Environmental Contaminants Act
through Parliament, which banned the production and use in
Canada of polychlorinated biphenyls (PCBs) and other persistent
toxins.

The other environmental issue of growing concern in those times
was oil—the potential threats to the arctic posed by offshore drilling
operations, and to coastal waters by tankers. After the OPEC crises of
the mid 1970s, there was talk about putting an oil port somewhere on
our west coast to receive tanker loads of crude from the Alaskan oil
fields at Prudhoe Bay. By late 1976, a consortium was proposing to
build an oil terminal at Kitimat, where petroleum from Alaska,
Indonesia and the Middle East could be off-loaded, then piped over
the mountains to Edmonton, from where it would flow south to the
US Midwest. Kitimat sits at the end of a long, narrow inlet that opens
into tempestuous Hecate Strait. The Exxon Valdez's day of infamy was
still a decade in the future, but we had already seen the effects of the
Torrey Canyon spill and other disasters, and the prospect of a tanker
going aground in those pristine fjords was enough to send a cold
shiver up the spine of most British Columbians and that certainly
included me. Romeo LeBlanc and Transport Minister Otto Lang

appointed a federal Commissioner of Inquiry, law professor Andrew R. Thompson of UBC, to look into the matter and make recommendations. That appointment would come back to haunt me when I was Minister of Environment.

In 1975, Jeanne Sauvé and the members of the standing committee went north to look at what the Americans were doing at Prudhoe Bay. We also visited Tuktoyaktuk in the Northwest Territories, where the oil companies were creating artificial islands as platforms for exploratory drilling in the Arctic Ocean. We were based at an exploration camp, and when we came back for supper after a day's touring, everyone immediately headed for the washrooms. But feminism had not yet made any noticeable impact on the frontier oil industry in those days, and Jeanne Sauvé soon discovered that there was no such thing as a woman's washroom in the Tuk camp. Being a good parliamentary secretary, I volunteered to guard the door to the men's room for my minister, but I warned her, "Jeanne, you may have to stand up for your rights."

I had less to do with Romeo LeBlanc's side of the department, though I assisted whenever I was asked. We spent a lot of time together touring the west coast, to familiarize ourselves with the realities of the BC fisheries. But Romeo was an old hand and had less need of a PS than Jeanne; still, he always included me on official occasions. On one of those occasions, I was invited to an evening reception in honour of a visiting Chinese fishing delegation, one of a flurry of official visits from what we used to call "Red" China that descended on Ottawa in the mid-1970s, after we recognized the government of one quarter of the world's people.

I went over to the Pearson Building for the usual toasts and handshakes. It had been a long day and I was tired, so when the formalities were done with, I sat down on the edge of a table off to one side. One of the Chinese delegates made a beeline for me and began to speak animatedly and at length in what I suppose was Mandarin. Over the years, this sort of thing has happened to me many times; I have been addressed in their own tongues by Chinese, Japanese, Filipinos, Indonesians and others I couldn't immediately identify. This time, however, I had the presence of mind to smile broadly and reply at equal length in Okanagan.

After I had served my two-year term as Parliamentary Secretary to Romeo LeBlanc and Jeanne Sauvé, I was briefly the chair of the Standing Committee on Indian Affairs and Northern Development. The big issue we wanted to deal with was the injustice done to Indian women who had lost their status by marrying non-Indians. But the residual ill feeling over the 1969 White Paper was still too strong among my people. The issue would have to wait until the Mulroney government introduced a bill in 1985, and it would be short on fundamentals, ending only some of the injustice.

Looking back, it was probably just as well that I didn't make it into the Cabinet right after the 1974 election, because my personal life was undergoing some devastating stresses in those years. My father had died in 1973, and in 1974 my mother's health began to decline, I believe because of the strain of caring for my father as he gradually succumbed to a neurological disorder that the doctors could not diagnose.

My father's death shook me down to my roots, even though it had clearly been coming for five years. The first signs that something was wrong had come in the fall of 1968. He had gone down to Nespelem in Washington State, where we had family, to lead the prayers at the funeral of his cousin, George Marchand. Suddenly, and for no apparent reason, he fell to the floor, unconscious.

I was in Ottawa, at a function organized by the Canadian JayCees to recognize Canada's "Very Outstanding Young Men." I remember that I was chatting with Newfoundland Premier Joey Smallwood and someone came to tell me that there was an urgent call from Donna; when I heard that my dad was ill, I went right home and packed, then caught the first flight west. I found my father in the Vernon hospital. The doctors had done some tests, and they suspected it was a neurological problem, but they couldn't find anything wrong with him. I took him home and he seemed fine, but from then on he would be struck occasionally by sudden blackouts. Once, while driving along the highway a few miles from Six Mile Creek, he passed out at the wheel. My mother, in the passenger seat, had to move fast to prevent the car from going off the road, then get them back home, though she had seldom driven a car before.

My dad was examined by our friend, Dr. Gur Singh, a neurologist in Kamloops. It seemed he was having a succession of mini-strokes that would render him unconscious but which did not leave him incapacitated. We had every kind of test they had, but no one could pinpoint the cause of his condition nor any way to treat or prevent it. Then gradually his condition worsened, and the doctors were not expecting him to get better. I couldn't stand not knowing what was wrong. I grew more and more angry, with the doctors, with myself, with everybody around me. Eventually, my mother could no longer cope—the stress of caring for him at home probably contributed to the onset of the cancer that would kill her in 1978—and we put dad in a nursing facility.

He died on July 15, 1978, and it was surely the worst day of my life. Perhaps because I could not cry for him, my emotion came out as a great, unfocused anger. The doctors wanted to perform an autopsy, to find out by the most direct methods what they had not been able to determine by tests. But I would not let them touch him; they hadn't been able to help him when he was trying to stay alive, so they could leave him be now that he was dead. I regret that emotional decision more than anything else I have done in my life, because now I will never know what killed my father.

There was a huge funeral on the reserve, with the church packed to overflowing. Joe Marchand had been a respected member of our community with many friends and relatives, and hundreds came to say goodbye. Pierre Trudeau sent flowers. So did the caucus and the party. The service was a Catholic mass, and the priest came around the day before to ask if we wanted to have the old hymns sung in Okanagan. I said no, make it as short a service as possible. It would have been too sad for us; we would not have been able to maintain our dignity. In these days of easy-flowing emotion, when the question most commonly asked by reporters is, "How do you feel?" our way of doing things may seem harsh. But I have no doubt that is how my father would have wanted it. He would have said, "Don't make a fool of yourself." We would not have honoured him by crying, just as he had never let us see him shed a tear.

But when it was over, and the guests had gone, I went out by myself and stood beside the fence in the darkness on the land that he and I had worked and ridden together. I thought of the times we had spent with each other during my growing up. I let myself think of the might-have-beens: though my father never learned to read or write, he was an intelligent man; there's no telling what he might have accomplished if that good mind of his had been offered an education and a decent chance in the world. I thought about all of that, and with no one there to see me, I let the tears come.

<hr>

It was Christmas of 1975, and Donna and I were just leaving the big Liberal holiday bash in Room 200 of the West Block. Pierre Trudeau saw us heading for the door and called us over. He said, "Margaret and I are going to be visiting Mexico, Cuba and Venezuela in the new year, and we'd like you and Donna to come along." Well, there's no better time to get out of Ottawa than January, when the deep cold settles in for what seems a permanent stay, so we were delighted to say yes.

The PM often made it a practice to take MPs with him on foreign state visits, as part of our education, so I didn't read too much into the invitation to travel. I was a fairly senior backbencher, so I supposed it was just my turn. But I also got a little nudge from a couple of people who suggested I be at my best on the trip, because the boss would be taking a close look at me to see if I measured up for consideration in the next cabinet shuffle.

We flew first to Mexico, and received the full red carpet treatment. Trudeau included me in all the formal talks with President Luis Echevarria, and I was seated at the head table for every luncheon and banquet. Many Mexicans have Indian ancestry, so I was not that much of a curiosity. Donna and Margaret had always gotten along and enjoyed themselves touring around Mexico City with the President's wife. The Trudeaus' third son, Michel, was a babe in Margaret's arms, and if anyone thought it unusual that a prime minister's wife would bring a baby along on a state visit, no one mentioned it. It's odd to think now that that little baby would not live to see more than young manhood, and my heart goes out to Pierre and Margaret for their loss.

After Mexico came Cuba. The reception at the Havana airport was overwhelming—thousands of people, maple leaf flags everywhere, a military band crashing through O Canada and people cheering as we walked down the red carpet to be greeted by Fidel Castro. Trudeau and I climbed into a jeep that had a rail mounted on it so we could stand in the back, and we drove across the tarmac to inspect the guard of honour. Pierre and Fidel were chatting away amiably in Spanish, with the PM pausing to translate for me, as we went up and down the rows of Cuban soldiers. "These are the ones we didn't send to Angola," Castro said, with deadpan humour, knowing that Cuba's military adventurism was one of the irritants that Canada had come to talk about.

We stayed in a little compound of luxurious buildings that had begun to run down; I still don't know if Castro was kidding when he said it used to be Frank Sinatra's summer retreat. The swimming pool was empty, but the cook provided by the Cuban government was excellent. I'd had plenty of pheasant back on the rez, but this was the first time I'd had it under glass. There was a definite difference.

Again, Trudeau brought me in to all of the meetings, except for whatever he and Castro talked about when they went skin diving together. The discussions on trade, aid and Angola, on the last of which the Prime Minister was very firm in expressing Canada's displeasure, were conducted in a Quonset hut that was first carefully swept for listening devices by Cuban technicians. When the space was declared free of bugs, Castro took off the pistol belt he always wore with his military fatigues and said, "I guess the CIA can't find me here." At some point, Trudeau mentioned that I was the first of my people elected to Parliament. "Ah, *Indio*," Castro said, nodding. Then he wrapped his arms around me in a bear hug. Iain Hunter, a reporter from the *Vancouver Sun*, joked, "Wait till I show these photos around Kamloops in your next campaign."

The Cubans had organized many events, and at some of them I represented Canada. I officiated at a performance by a visiting

Canadian ballet company, and toured a model dairy farm stocked with Canadian Holsteins that was a particular favourite of Ramón Castro, the President's elder brother and Cuba's Minister of Agriculture: a big, shambling man, devoted to the care of his cows, who reminded me of Eugene Whelan. "Every Cuban child has milk every day," Fidel told us, as well as good health care and free education. We visited a school, and there was no doubt how the kids felt about him. Sure, the reception at the airport was staged, and so was the big rally at Cienfuegos where fifty thousand or more people packed a soccer stadium to hear Castro speak for three hours straight, shouting *"Viva Canada"* and *"Viva Cuba"* on cue. But the looks on the faces of the teenagers at that school as they crowded around *El Presidente* were genuine adoration; my daughter Lori might have looked the same if she'd had a visit from the Beatles.

I'd read up on Cuba before the trip. I knew what things had been like under Fulgencio Battista, the dictator that Castro's revolutionaries had driven from power. There would not have been too many glasses of milk or free dental care for the poor kids back then. They would have received only the same horrifically casual disdain that I heard expressed by a government official at our next stop, in Caracas, Venezuela.

The differences between Venezuela and Cuba were evident the moment we stepped off the plane at the national airport. White gloved officials quickly shooed all of us except for Pierre and Margaret off the red carpet. No one but the Prime Minister was invited to the talks with the Venezuelan President. In the supposed police state of Cuba, we had stayed in a house with only a maid and a cook to look after us; in democratic Caracas, we were kept in an army barracks, with submachine gun toting soldiers all around—in case the guerrillas come down from the mountains, we were told.

At an official luncheon hosted by the Venezuelan president, I sat next to the Minister of Education. I asked about the barrios of tarpaper shacks we had seen clinging to the hillsides as we drove in from the airport. Many of the people living in them had faces the same colour as mine; they were destitute *indios* who had come to the city hoping to find jobs and an escape from poverty. The Venezuelan

Minister, whose ancestors had been Spanish colonials, considered the barrio dwellers to be not worth discussing. I suggested that education was the solution, but he waved away the idea. "We don't try to educate them," he said. "They're not capable of learning." I thought about those kids hanging on Fidel Castro's arms. I thought about my father and all his generation left to rot in ignorance. But I bit my tongue—I was representing my country as well as my people, and there was no point in creating an international incident by explaining to that offensive and pompous fool just how viciously wrong he was.

Forbearing to rip a strip off foreign dignitaries may have been one of the tests Pierre Trudeau liked his backbenchers to pass before he took them into cabinet. If so, I appeared to have aced it. On September 13, 1976, having first received a tipoff from PMO to expect a summons from the Prime Minister, the call to Cabinet finally came. But it was not the job I had been told to expect.

"I wanted to put you into National Revenue," Pierre said, when I sat across the desk from him in his Langevin Block office. It was almost evening, and I had been hanging around my office all afternoon, waiting for his call. "I know you'd like Agriculture or Environment"—we'd talked about both of those jobs at one time or another—"but I can't offer you either of them this time." We had long since talked about Indian Affairs, and we'd agreed that I could never accept it. I would have been a sitting-duck target for every radical; the expectations of moderate Indians would have gone through the roof, and I would never have been able to satisfy half of them. I'd been expecting National Revenue, one of the traditional break-in points for rookie ministers, so it was a surprise when Pierre said he couldn't put me there.

"I'm sorry to be so late in getting to you," he said, "but Mackasey has just resigned." Labour Minister Bryce Mackasey had apparently gotten upset about something and impulsively walked out of cabinet just as the PM was trying to put it together. Pierre said he had had to put Toronto MP Tony Abbott into Mackasey's vacated slot, instead of into the newly created post of Minister of State for Small Business.

Would I be willing to take on the small business job? Well, of course I would. I'm not immune to the normal temptations of any politician, and the potential for a good public profile was a lot better in the new ministry than it would have been if I'd been the nation's chief tax collector.

I can't say I knew a lot about small business, but the job, as Pierre Trudeau outlined it, was essentially a question of developing a policy from the ground up. In other words, it was a research assignment: go and find out what Canadian small business people needed and come back with some recommendations on how we could give it to them. That suited me fine—if there's one thing I know how to do, it's field research. As an add-on, Pierre made me the minister responsible for metric conversion; I guess he figured that, being a scientist, I already knew my way around a decimal.

I gathered together a good staff. As executive assistant—that's Ottawa jargon for a minister's chief of staff—I recruited former Kamloopsian Roy Derrick, a very able and experienced Hill veteran, who was then doing the same job for Ron Basford. It wasn't a case of

Official Cabinet photo with Her Majesty, Queen Elizabeth in 1977.

rustling from a colleague's herd; Ron had been made Minister of Justice in 1975 and was finding that he needed a lawyer as the head of his staff. From Ray Perrault's office came Jim Davidson to be my political assistant. Jim had been a firebrand of a campaigner in my riding since his university days, and he had lived in our basement for a while when he had first come to Ottawa to take a researcher's job. Brenda Eaton, from a staunch Liberal family in Victoria, was hired as my constituency assistant. Ron Basford's speech writer, whose name also appears on the cover of this book, came over to be my communications aide. Louise Branch was my assistant for Parlimentary issues. My secretary was Terri Selbee.

In later years my staff went on to good careers. After working in strategic planning and communications with the RoyalDutch/Shell Group in Canada and in South Africa, Roy Derrick is today the director of public affairs for the Regina Health District. Jim Davidson is the regional communications coordinator for the BC Ministry of Transportation and Highways in the southern Interior. Brenda Eaton made a career in the BC civil service, eventually resigning as Deputy Minister of Finance rather than to yield to NDP pressure to cook the government's books. Louise Branch is in charge of the Asian trade desk at External Affairs.

We set up a ministerial office in a nondescript building on Albert Street in downtown Ottawa, and established a connection with the Department of Industry, Trade and Commerce (IT&C). Being a Minister of State, I did not have my own department, but received all my resources on loan from IT&C, which was then headed by Jean Chrétien. The Deputy Minister, O.G. Stoner, was subsequently replaced by Gordon Osbaldeston, a very senior member of the civil service establishment. IT&C lent us an assistant deputy minister and some other officials; we formed them into a Small Business Secretariat within the larger department and set to work.

The Secretariat commissioned studies and research papers, and began setting up a series of public consultations with small business people all across the country. Eventually, I travelled to every province, meeting with small groups of business owners and operators and asking them two basic questions; what should government be doing to help you, and what are we doing now that's getting in your way? As I expected, we sometimes got some blunt answers. We weren't "rounding up the usual suspects" —the kind of people who always seem to be presenting their views and demands to government—but listening to ordinary folks who were trying to make their way in the world. There was one "usual suspect" in the mix, however: John Bullock, the President of the Canadian Federation of Independent Business; John supported what we were trying to do, and was always an able and helpful source of advice.

I considered these consultations—augmented by a fair amount of speechmaking and talking to the media—a useful exercise in bringing government closer to the people. And the whole effort appeared to strike a chord with the public: a few months into the job, our internal polls showed that the small business initiative was the most popular thing the government had going for it. Ironically, however, we were subject to constant foot-dragging by the department, including the senior officials who were supposed to be helping us create a small business policy.

It was nothing blatant or obvious, and it was much more evident to my staff than it was to me. But it reminded me of the time when Art Laing and I had wanted to help the Hurons buy more land, only to be told it was "not departmental policy" to add to Indian reserves. It eventually became clear that small business was not a big priority among the upper echelons of the Department of Industry, Trade and Commerce; as one of the most senior officers of the department expressed it to my executive assistant, there was no such thing as small business; small firms were merely the "service centre" for big business in Canada.

Big business was what IT&C was established to deal with. Its top bureaucrats were accustomed to hobnobbing with the suits on Bay Street, and piddling about with small business people was not a particularly good route into the upper circle for an ambitious IT&C bureaucrat. So it couldn't be said that the government's small business initiative attracted the department's best and brightest, nor that they gave their best to the cause of helping their fellow Canadians who ran mom-and-pop stores or small manufacturing companies.

Nonetheless, by dint of some heroic efforts by my personal staff—including one memorable meeting between Roy Derrick and the unmotivated IT&C officials on loan to us, during which my executive assistant shouted so loudly he temporarily lost his voice—we got the research job done. We issued a discussion paper called Small Business In Canada: Perspectives, which was mostly written in my ministerial office. To prevent the IT&C operatives from messing around with or delaying the document, Roy Derrick had it printed by the Secure Unit of the Queen's Printer in Hull, the section that handles budgets and other top secret material. Despite the "active disinterest" of the departmental hierarchs, we managed to put through Cabinet Canada's first comprehensive federal policy toward the small business sector. It was well received.

I must say that I took to being a minister. I was ready for the responsibility, having come a long way in the eleven years since I had boarded the train to be an assistant to Jack Nicholson and Art Laing, an experience which taught me a lot about how a minister's office should run. I especially learned from Art Laing to have respect for the public's dollar. The first Christmas I was in his office as an assistant, I discovered that he never used the MP's "franking" privileges to send out personal mail like Christmas cards, although most MPs and ministers routinely did. "When you're sitting where the buck stops, you have to know who you are," he told me. "You have to divide your private interest from your public duty." My staff thought I was a little too mean with the pennies—all those who came to my office from other ministers' staffs took pay cuts—but that's the way I am.

I was quiet and workmanlike in Cabinet meetings. I had no turf to protect and no ambitions to replace the man sitting in the big chair. Pierre Trudeau has somehow acquired the image of an autocrat in Cabinet, but he was in fact the best chairman of any committee in which I have ever sat. He listened closely to the arguments of competing ministers, and played no favourites. You could always have your say with Trudeau, but you'd better be saying something worth listening to—he was unforgiving to any minister who came to Cabinet unprepared to argue his case. And he liked the discussions to remain collegial; if a minister let a little acid creep into his tone, I sensed that the boss was mentally putting a demerit mark next to that minister's name.

One small aside: it was during my one-year term as small business minister that I gave what Donna has always called the finest speech of my career. Actually, it was only a segment of a standard "road speech" on small buisness affairs that I was invited to give to a meeting of western regional newspaper publishers in Banff in the spring of 1977, and it was about national unity. With the election of the first Parti Québecois government six months earlier, the whole country had become gripped by the prospect of Québec secession. Word had come from PMO to all ministers that every speech, no matter what the subject or whom the audience, was to include a reference to the issue of national unity.

As an Indian, born into a country that had denied me citizenship until I was twenty-six years old, I think I had a different slant on Québec separation than most Canadians. I wanted my obligatory handling of the national unity issue to reflect my background. And I wanted it to be a personal statement, from the heart. So, midway through my speech on small business to the publishers, I said:

"I would like to digress for a moment to talk about an issue that is of great importance to all Canadians—including westerners, and I'm one.

"I can get emotional about the prospect of my country being dismembered. Apart from the dollars and cents issues—the war of accounts, someone has called it—the possibility that my country could be diminished by the loss of a large part of its territory gives me a strong gut reaction. I don't want to see it happen.

"My ancestors have been in this country a long time. My people have not always enjoyed the best of treatment from Canadian society, although that has changed greatly in the last generation. But I consider myself a Canadian, first and forever. Québec is a part of my national heritage, just as much a part as the Cariboo, or the Prairies or the Maritimes.

"I know there are people in the west who say, 'let them go.' Well, I say, 'No way. No way are you going to take my country—or any part of it—from me.'

"I am ready to make accommodations. I am ready to look at any proposal that will make my country a better place for my children to grow up

in. But there is no way that I could ever turn to my son and daughter and say, 'Sorry, kids, but it was all too much trouble to keep Canada united.'

"I am sure that none of you here today would want to have to say the same thing to your own children."

And that was about it. I asked them, as community newspaper publishers, to make sure that their readers had the facts on what was happening within our country, and that they try to foster a spirit of tolerance between east and west. Then I went on to talk some more about small business policy. As I look at my words now, in black and white, they don't seem all that compelling. But when I had finished that little segment of my speech, there was a burst of applause. I looked up and saw tears in the eyes of some of those small-town newspaper owners. I've thought about that day from time to time, especially when I've heard the likes of Jacques Parizeau blustering on

At a meeting on Small Business with John Bullock, Pres. Canadian Federation of Independent Business, and the Hon. Donald MacDonald, Minister of Finance. 1976 "They were tall."

about Canada not being "a real country." I bet he wouldn't have cared to say such a thing in that hotel ballroom in Banff. We don't stick out our chests and we don't wave flags, but down deep there's a raw emotion about this country. It means something to be a Canadian.

Through the summer of 1977, we put together a discussion paper and policy submission for Cabinet, and got it through the complex approval process. It was a good paper—credit for which goes solidly to my staff, and certainly not to the on-loan officials from IT&C—and the measures we were proposing for the benefit of small business were popular, so I did not have to fight very hard to get it approved. The new small business policy was scheduled to be announced at the annual general meeting of the Canadian Chamber of Commerce in Edmonton on September 19. I had a speech prepared for the

Addressing a joint meeting of Canadian and American Foresters in St. Louis, Missouri, July 1978, as Federal Minister of Forestry.

announcement, but I never delivered it. It was delivered instead by Tony Abbott, because a few days before the Chamber's AGM, Pierre Trudeau reshuffled his Cabinet and made me Minister of Environment.

This shuffle was a more orderly business. The PM had me in for a chat, told me he liked what I'd done in Small Business, and asked me how I felt about taking on Environment. I told him I felt just great about it: it was one of the two departments I'd always wanted, although technically it wasn't yet a stand-alone department. I would be Minister of State, Environment, and Romeo LeBlanc would be Minister of State, Fisheries, until the two components disentangled themselves from each other.

The separating of Environment from Fisheries made a land war in Asia look comparatively simple, as well-entrenched bureaucratic empires mobilized against each other, and heads of directorates and assistant deputy ministers in charge of services fought by memo and meeting to keep their establishments from being broken up. The civil service hierarchy works the same in Ottawa as anywhere else: the more people you have reporting to you, the more important you are; if someone takes away too many of your subordinates, you may lose your place in the pecking order.

I stayed well away from that morass, and had no disagreements with Romeo about the division of labour. He was much more interested in Fisheries, and left Environment to me, even though one of the first hot issues I had to deal with was centred in his home province: the apparent connection between the fatal children's disease, Reye's Syndrome, and aerial pesticide spraying to eradicate a spruce budworm infestation in the New Brunswick forests. Fortunately, Environment Canada, as the federal agency responsible for forestry research, was leading the way in finding an alternative to pesticides.

One of the department's scientists, Dr. Vladimir Smirnoff, was conducting research in the Québec City regional office into a promising non-chemical, biological control for spruce budworm. The agent was a naturally occurring bacterium called *Bacillus thuringiensis* which took up residence in the intestines of any caterpillar that ingested it and quickly killed the host. If Bt, as it was usually referred to, could be introduced into the guts of enough spruce budworms, it would wipe out vast populations of the pest, but would be harmless to other wildlife in the forests. Dr. Smirnoff was working on new and better ways to deliver this natural insect control system, and one of the first things I did as Minister of Environment was to make sure his research was well funded. In time, he came through with a delivery system that allowed Bt to be applied by aerial or hand-held spray, and because of his work and Environment Canada's support, I can walk into Sandy McCurrach's feedstore today and find this natural pest control method for sale in a commercial version.

There were bigger issues building around the environment portfolio in those days. We knew that something was going wrong in the eastern woodlands. Trees were dying, and the maple sugar industry was threatened. The acid levels in lakes and ponds had been creeping up for years. Scientists were pointing the finger at sulphur emissions from industrial smokestacks and especially from thermal energy plants that burned low grade coal with a high sulphur content. The sulphur combined with water molecules in the atmosphere to form a weak solution of sulphuric acid, which fell with the rain that had been refilling lakes and seeping into groundwater for generations. The phrase "acid rain" had moved from the labs into the newspapers and from there into the political arena.

Romeo LeBlanc had already called acid rain a ticking time bomb waiting to go off. We were already seeing dead lakes and thinning woodlands in eastern Canada and the New England states, but the political will to tackle the problem was most lacking where it was most needed—down in the US. It was true that the big stack at Inco's Sudbury smelter complex and the steel mills of Hamilton were a serious part of the problem, but the major source of the acid rain blight was the industrial heartland of the US northeast—all those coal-burning mills and generating plants that would soon be collectively relabelled the "rust belt." But those plants made profits and taxes and sustained jobs, and against that reality, the threat of sickly trees and sterile lakes—especially north of the border—didn't mean much to your average US Congressman.

So Canada had a double challenge: we had to do the scientific research that would delineate the extent and origins of the problem— what tree species were affected, and how, the effects on soils, and so on—and we also had to convince the United States that the problem was real in the first place, and that it was worth solving. I am proud to say that I began the efforts that eventually led to success in both spheres, although as recently declassified records from the US government reveal, the American decision to take heed of Canada's concerns over acid rain was based on their perceived need to throw Brian Mulroney a "sop" after he had flip-flopped on free trade, and gave the Americans what they had always wanted—but had never been able to get—from every previous Canadian government since Confederation.

I was aware that I was barely getting the ball rolling on acid rain research, but I have to admit that I was having a wonderful time. Environment Canada was chock full of scientists—most of them, like me, from the life sciences—and I had plenty of opportunities to talk the talk again. I also renewed acquaintanceship with a number of people from my pre-political days: one of my old UBC profs, Dr. Ian MacTaggart-Cowan, was a member of my Minister's Advisory Board; another, Professor Vernon C. (Bert) Brink, was on a special advisory panel looking for solutions to the problem posed by birds on the flight path at Vancouver International Airport. Dr. David Munro, Director of the Canadian Wildlife Service, which was part of Environment Canada, was an old UBC grad who hailed from Kalamalka Lake. And Dr. John Tener, who replaced Dave Munro, was another fellow British Columbian who had started out in a one-room school in the little town of Falkland, in my riding.

Issues like acid rain and spruce budworm were files that were already active when I stepped into the Environment portfolio, but there was one big item that I wanted to add to the department's agenda, and I got started as soon as I had my feet under the minister's desk. For some time, I had been growing deeply concerned over the declining state of Canada's forests, particularly the fact that forest management in our country amounted to little more than cutting down the trees and letting God grow them back again. In 1976, people like the Swedes and the New Zealanders were scientifically tending their forests for maximum yield—both in timber volumes and in jobs—but in Canada the concept of intensive forest management was not even in its infancy. As the minister responsible for the Canadian Forestry Service and all federal efforts to support forestry research, I wanted to do something about that.

One thing I could do right away was to use my position as a platform to make people take notice of the poor condition of the country's forests. These days, when companies like Weyerhaeuser commit themselves to end clearcutting and promote biodiversity in the forests, it may be hard for younger Canadians to realize that only twenty years ago, the key word in the phrase "forest industry" was *industry*. Most of the people who made the key decisions about what to do with Canada's forests—both in government and in the corporate world—had been trained as engineers. To them, the challenges facing the industry were questions of production, questions that began with the arrival of a log at the mill and ended with a stack of two-by-fours in the lumber yard. The fact that vast stretches of mature forest in my home province of British Columbia had been cut down and left to grow "weed" species like alder did not register on their narrow-focus radar screens. Neither did the fact that our overseas competitors were getting way more value—both in product and in jobs—out of a cubic metre of wood than we were, even though ours was premium fibre.

So I made speeches and I encouraged my officials to get out and pitch for intensive forestry wherever they could. I lobbied hard to get more support from the Canadian government for forestry research, both in the universities and in specialized research institutions like Vancouver's Forintek. And I found I could apply a little leverage in the spending of federal dollars through the Special ARDA (Agricultural Research and Development Agreements) program of the Department of Regional Economic Expansion (DREE). Special ARDA was a federal-provincial cooperative endeavour that funnelled federal money into economically depressed rural areas. The provinces administered the programs, and used the cash for forest-related

Special ARDA projects for building logging roads, which often opened up new areas for harvesting operations, and thus created jobs. But, since Ottawa was providing a lot of the spending, and since my Canadian Forestry Service staff helped negotiate the agreements for the federal government, I saw an opportunity to reorient the purpose of the projects toward better forest management. With the agreement of Marcel Lessard, the Minister of DREE, we set about redefining the thrust of Special ARDA to include commercial thinning of second-growth stands, trimming trees to promote better trunk growth, fertilizing and other intensive forest management techniques.

Considering the state of the forests in British Columbia, where vast stretches of once productive timberlands were officially categorized in 1977 as Not Satisfactorily Restocked—meaning the prime Douglas fir or Sitka spruce had been cut, but only weed trees had sprung up to replace them—you would have thought that the provincial government would have welcomed the help. But relations between Victoria and Ottawa have always been characterized by a certain degree of paranoia on the part of BC, and that pathological suspicion was in full flower in the mind of Premier Bill Bennett's Minister of Forests, Tom Waterland.

The forests, like all natural resources, are a provincial area of jurisdiction. It says so in the British North America Act. As the Canadian minister responsible for forestry research, I wanted to promote the practice of more intensive forest management, and I was using the federal spending power to nudge provincial forest ministries in that healthy direction. From this, Tom Waterland somehow concluded that I was attempting to wrest control of the forest resource from his hands so that I could run it from Ottawa. He ran to the BC press, which was always much more sympathetic to provincial Social Credit than to the federal Liberals, and began to whip up a public fuss about it. Behind the scenes, my departmental officials were trying to reassure Waterland's officials that he was very far off base. But the BC Ministry of Forests had come to count on that federal money for road building, and the ministry had its own reasons for going along with the minister's paranoid charade. After we had been down every conceivable avenue of persuasion and found that it dead-ended at the

Turning sod for a new Senior Citizens' facility in Vernon, B,C. with Premier Bill Bennet summer, 1977.

provincial minister's intransigence, the problem was resolved by the application of some brute political arm-twisting: there were certain other federal programs under which BC was expecting considerable largess from Ottawa, money that Bill Bennett was counting on, and the Premier was informed that those funds were in jeopardy unless he reined in his Minister of Forests and had him sign the Special ARDA agreement. Mr. Waterland's objections evaporated—at least pub-licly—and BC moved a step or two closer to having a modern forest sector.

During the Bill Bennett years, the MLA for Kamloops was Rafe Mair, who is now the dean of BC's open-line radio hosts. Although Rafe was a Social Crediter, he belonged to the Tory side of the Socred-Conservative-Liberal coalition that Bill Bennett put together to drive Dave Barrett and the NDP from office. I often heard it said that no federal Conservative could get that party's nomination in Kamloops unless he had Rafe Mair's blessing. Given our allegiances, it was no wonder that the MLA often took cheap shots at the MP, or that the MP snarled back in kind. But, overall, I think we developed a healthy respect for each other.

One thing I will credit Rafe Mair for: he treated my people fairly. For example, for many years the imposition of provincial taxation on businesses operating from leases on Kamloops reserve land was a scandal. The province collected property taxes from businesses that held leases from the Kamloops Band, not to mention sales tax and other levies, but not one penny of that money went into services for the area, as it would have if the businesses hadn't been on Indian land. It turned out that the Province was making more money from those businesses than the Band was, although the Band had to build roads and put in water and sewers and other municipal-type services. But when Rafe Mair went into the provincial cabinet, he put that situation right. He also reversed an earlier NDP government move that had included the reserve within the redrawn boundaries of the City of Kamloops.

I have left to the end of this chapter the events that constitute, I believe, not just the most important accomplishment of my time as Canada's Minister of Environment, but the most significant achievement of my whole career in public life: quashing the attempt to put an oil port on the coast of British Columbia. In order to do it, I had to perform a little skullduggery to deal with a federal Commissioner of Inquiry who appeared to have gone way out of orbit.

As mentioned earlier, UBC law professor Andrew R. Thompson (no relation to Senator Andrew Thompson whose non-attendance record became a scandal), was appointed in March 1977 to inquire into the environmental, social and navigational safety implications of a proposal to create an oil port at Kitimat, at the end of Douglas Channel. Crude from Alaska and other overseas oil fields would be piped from there to Edmonton, then on to the US. By late May, Dr. Thompson was staffed and budgeted and ready to get to work. But that was just in time for the oil port proponent, Kitimat Pipe Line Ltd. (KPL), to ask the National Energy Board to hold its application "in abeyance." The reason: Trans Mountain Pipe Line Company (TMPL) had come up with a competing proposal that would have seen tankers coming in to Cherry Point, in Washington State, and sending their crude to Edmonton via the existing TMPL pipe.

Cabinet revisited the Order in Council that had set up the Kitimat

Rusins cartoon in the Ottawa Citizen 1978. As Environment Minister, I urged our government to lead the way in paper recycling.

Oil Port Inquiry and amended it to allow Dr. Thompson to study the potential impacts of west coast oil ports in general. The Commissioner shifted gears and proceeded to conduct what was now called the "West Coast Oil Ports Inquiry." But the whole business was moving far too slowly, and the costs were climbing. There was no chance the Commissioner could have a report ready for the Government of Canada by the date that had originally been set down in the Order in Council, December 31, 1977. And as the show rolled on into the fall, he had already pretty well spent his $1.4 million budget but still had plans to hold several more community hearings up and down the BC coast.

Then things got more complicated when the US Congress passed an amendment to its Marine Mammals Protection Act, and President Jimmy Carter declined to veto it. The amendment effectively killed Trans Mountain's hopes of putting an oil terminal at Cherry Point. Now the West Coast Oil Ports Inquiry was up and running, spending money it didn't really have, when there wasn't really an oil port proposal for it to consider. Meanwhile, all the interest groups, from fishermen to urban environmentalists, were clamoring to keep the inquiry going, because it was providing them with a high-profile platform from which to push their causes, and funds in the form of intervenor subsidies from the inquiry budget.

The Commissioner came to Ottawa in November to meet with Romeo LeBlanc and Otto Lang. He had already written to them asking for an extension of his mandate and a $2 million increase in his budget, to both of which requests the Ministers had said no. So the meeting got a little heated: the Commissioner essentially told the Ministers that he would make a very loud and very public fuss if he was not allowed to continue with his appointment. The impression LeBlanc and Lang received was that Dr. Thompson would tell the media that the Inquiry had been a sham, that the ministers had used him as a smokescreen to disguise their intent to go ahead with an oil port on the west coast. At the end of the day, however, there was a compromise: Dr. Thompson would recess the inquiry and prepare a "Statement of Proceedings" reporting on his findings up to December 31. His mandate would be extended to March 31, 1978, and he would have some extra funding—it worked out to $300,000—for his intervenors.

But, in that meeting, the two ministers made a serious mistake. They agreed—and publicly announced—that the Commissioner could reactivate his inquiry if another oil port proposal—like the KPL application that was still "in abeyance"—were filed with the NEB. The mistake was that Romeo LeBlanc and Otto Lang did not have the legal authority to promise the Commissioner he could bring his inquiry back to life whenever he chose to do so, regardless of the terms of the Order in Council that said he was out of business on March 31, 1978. Taxpayers' money cannot be spent by a Commission of Inquiry without a lawful process involving a vote of Treasury Board and an Order in Council approved by the Cabinet, neither of which were likely to be forthcoming. The two ministers had agreed to grant a private citizen the powers that belong to the government as a whole, and they had no right to do that.

In mid December, Dr. Thompson wound up his inquiry to that

date and began to write his Statement of Proceedings. Shortly after, a new Order in Council was prepared, granting him more money, but not the authority to revive the inquiry at his discretion. The Cabinet merely ordered LeBlanc and Lang to consult with the Commissioner if a new oil port proposal appeared in 1978. Dr. Thompson, quite rightly, felt that the government had reneged on the November agreement, and said so in correspondence with the ministers. The dispute would have remained academic, if KPL hadn't popped up in January 1978, asking to have its application put back on the NEB's agenda. The Commissioner was not long in demanding that his inquiry be reactivated, and the government was suddenly in a bind.

Nobody in his right mind wanted an oil port on the west coast. If Dr. Thompson had been able to review the original Kitimat Pipe Line Proposal in a few months, as planned, the Government of Canada could have blown the idea out of the water and got on with other matters. But the stops and starts and shifts of direction—plus the two ministers' error of agreeing to something they couldn't deliver—had caused the whole thing to get out of control. The Commissioner was now convinced he had been played for a patsy. The activist groups and people in coastal communities were in an uproar. And, worst of all, it looked as if we would be riding this runaway train straight into a spring election.

Something needed to be done, so we did it. Fortunately, I had a good personal staff: all the people I had hired when I first became a minister, now joined at Environment Canada by Sally Bennett, another former political assistant to Ron Basford. Together, with some very expert manoeuvering by my Executive Assistant, Roy Derrick, we concocted and carried through a slightly devious plan. We led Dr. Thompson to believe that it would take a fair amount of time to translate his Statement of Proceedings, after he provided us with a draft, so that it could go to Cabinet in both official languages for a decision. In fact, we had the report translated very quickly, so it could form the basis for a submission to Cabinet that asked for a decision quite different from what the Commissioner expected.

I have to admit that we let Dr. Thompson believe that we would not be going to Cabinet with his report until after he formally delivered it to us in late February. We also did not disabuse him of the belief that the question we would put to Cabinet would be whether or not to extend his mandate and give him more money. I believe he thought he had us over a barrel, and that we would grant his wishes rather than face the strong criticisms he would level against the government if we failed to meet his expectations.

But the Cabinet submission we prepared asked the Government to decide something else entirely: to declare that we saw no need for an oil port on the west coast, and didn't expect the country to need one in the foreseeable future. It was a clear signal to Kitimat Pipe Line that its application to the National Energy Board was a non-starter. And it meant that there was no need for a Commissioner of Inquiry to review, at increasing cost—both in terms of taxpayers' money and political damage to the Government—a development that was just never going to happen.

The Cabinet document was produced in record time. Normally, they evolve through several slow drafts prepared by painstaking civil servants, but Roy Derrick was a seasoned pro and knew how to put a good one together. Even so, it was touch and go for a while. The Cabinet committee process was not so easily hurried, and there were deadlines that had to be met, or the decision would not be made in time for D-Day—the February 23 date on which Dr. Thompson would present his report to the Government and release it simultaneously to the media.

At the last moment, the wheels almost fell off. Pierre Trudeau had set the rules for submissions to Cabinet: they not only had to be signed by the minister responsible for the particular area of policy, but they must also be co-signed by the minister who was politically responsible for the geographical area that was affected. The "political minister" for Kitimat and BC's middle and northern coast was the Minister of State for Fitness and Amateur Sports, Iona Campagnolo. The evening before the morning that would be the last chance to get the cab doc into the decision-making process of Cabinet, my staff met with one of Iona's senior aides. A copy of the document had earlier gone to her office for review, and her approval was expected. After all, this was the most contentious issue in her riding, and suspicion among the electorate that Ottawa meant to foist oil tanker traffic on the west coast after the election was likely to be fatal to her re-election and the prospects of any other coastal Liberal candidate between the Alaska Panhandle and the 49th Parallel.

Which was why it came as a shock to my staff when her assistant said, "Iona will sign this cab doc if you really insist," but she would have preferred to keep the issue open so she could go back to the riding and campaign against the threat of oil tankers on the coast. He said Iona wanted to tell the voters of Skeena riding that only she could prevent an oil port from happening. My staff made it clear that we intended to "really insist." In all likelihood, this was just a wild idea cooked up by her staff; certainly, Iona never suggested anything of the sort to me. The cab doc duly came back with her signature. I then took it to Cabinet and pushed it through.

On February 23, 1978, Dr. Andrew Thompson was in Ottawa to formally present his *Statement of Proceedings of the West Coast Oil Ports Inquiry* to my colleagues and me. He then went directly across Wellington Street to the National Press Building, and gave a press conference in which he threw down the gauntlet, almost daring the Government of Canada not to continue his mandate. He then went to the airport to catch a plane back to Vancouver, which is why he did not see me arrive at the National Press Theatre shortly after to hold my own press conference. I told the media and the people of Canada that there would be no oil port, no oil tankers, and no oil spills on the coast of British Columbia. The wording of the press release carried the phrasing from the Cabinet decision—"for the foreseeable future"—but I put it more bluntly: "No oil port. No way."

I suppose it was not nice to mislead a federal Commissioner of Inquiry. But politics is often an adversarial business, and Dr. Thompson was taking on the Government of Canada in a way that might have harmed the careers of my colleagues—ministers, MPs and candidates—who had no desire to see oil spreading on BC's beaches. So we contrived to resolve the issue quickly, if not without some manoeuvering.

As it turned out, none of those coastal candidates nor Iona nor I survived the election when it finally came in 1979. Ironically, the

Ottawa Citizen, Rusins Cartoon 1978, after Canada signed an agreement with the United States to clean up the Great Lakes.

only Liberal left standing was rookie Art Phillips in Vancouver Centre, who had earlier been courted by the Tories. But it doesn't matter now that we did not secure the election by killing the oil port proposal; what matters is that we preserved the coast of British Columbia from the inevitable horror show that struck Prince William Sound eleven years later.

I am not especially proud of the skullduggery that moved the cabinet document to a final decision, but I am very proud that I stopped an oil port from being foisted on the coast of British Columbia.

———

My mother had been diagnosed with bowel cancer in 1976. They operated, but it was too late: the cancer was already spreading through her system. But she was not in great discomfort most of the

time. The painkillers she took seemed to help, and she drank a tea
that she brewed up from saskatoon twigs, an old standby remedy
among us Okanagans. Throughout 1977 and into the spring of 1978,
she gradually weakened, and on April 14, she died in the Vernon hospital. Her funeral was like my father's, short and simple.

I regret that I never brought my parents to Ottawa, to see the big
stone buildings where I worked and where I was treated with dignity
and even some deference. But I was always so busy, and there was
never much money around when I was raising two kids on an MP's
salary, which is not that much. By the time I was making good money
as a minister, my father was dead and my mother was too ill to come
east.

Now I wish I had made the effort. To have walked my parents
through Parliament, shown them my office and my staff, taken them
for a meal in the restaurant and introduced them to the Prime
Minister—that would be a memory to cherish.

In the Ashcroft Stampede Parade, July, 1978—Appoloosa horse courtesy of the High School Principal, Mr. Crider, and photo by Roberta Derrick.

CHAPTER 6

"Go back to the reserve..."

O n a clear, cold day in February, 1979, I went to see Pierre Trudeau at 24 Sussex Drive. My daughter, Lori, who had just turned seventeen, came with me. After talking it over with Donna and the kids, I had decided it was time to look for another line of work, a difficult decision made easier by the knowledge that the majority of committed voters in my riding had already come to the same conclusion.

Pierre received me as graciously as ever. I am sure he was not surprised by what I had come to say. I told him that I was not leaving because of him, that I supported him completely and thought he was one of Canada's greatest prime ministers. But I had my family to think of, with two teenagers just coming up to the expensive post-secondary education phase of child-rearing, and that I thought it would be easier to line up a job while I was an incumbent minister and MP, rather than to wait until I was a defeated candidate. What I didn't say, but I'm sure he already knew, was that I didn't want to slog through the misery of a doomed campaign.

We were surely going to be defeated. All of my campaign team, Merv Chertkow, Sandy McCurrach, Don Andrews, Jim Davidson, were reporting a steady stream of gloomy indicators. And I knew from virtually every encounter with voters when I visited the riding that we were heading for the cliff's edge. I got the same disheartening message from constituents on Victoria Street in downtown Kamloops or outside the post office in little Falkland: "Sorry, Len. We like you, but we've got to get that s.o.b. Trudeau out."

It didn't matter that I had been a good MP, that I had swung the small end of the federal funding funnel toward my riding so that we got our share and then some of federal largesse: new post offices in Ashcroft, Salmon Arm, Blue River, Barriere, Clearwater, Chase, Falkland, and a new sub-post office in Kamloops; new RCM Police stations in Falkland, Ashcroft and Merritt, the latter opened after I left office; a new airport terminal and runway upgrade for Kamloops; the new KXA buildings, the Merritt airport improvements, and a slew of grants for student jobs, and projects under Special ARDA, RIP, RRAP and all the other acronyms of that free-spending time. The fifty-one jobs created by the establishment of the $800,000 Kamloops Disease Control Centre were forgotten history. If post offices won elections, I would have been a shoo-in. But none of that counted in my riding in 1979.

What counted was capital punishment, gun control, French on federal signs, and the perception of Trudeau's arrogance and disdain toward Canadians west of the Lakehead. That old "Why should I sell your wheat?" remark, knowingly and unfairly taken out of its Socratic context by conservative editorial writers all over western Canada, kept coming back as a club to beat us.

There had been a free vote in the House on capital punishment. Three of British Columbia's eight Liberal MPs—Ron Basford, Mark Raines and I—had voted for abolition and that was a vote that many of my constituents would neither forget nor forgive. It did no good to argue that, pragmatically, hanging was manifestly no deterrent to murder. (In England, when the noose was still in use, it was a common epithet to say, "I'll swing for you," meaning, "I'll kill you and hang for it.") And the principled arguments—that incompetence and injustice, as in the Donald Marshall case, would inevitably result in the execution of innocents, or that if it was wrong for a citizen to take a life it was no less wrong for the state to do so—cut no ice.

The reaction against gun control was even more ferocious, no doubt because many more of my constituents owned guns than were likely to be victims of murder—although, statistically, there was a definite correlation. Ron Basford, as Justice Minister, had brought in a package of rules that tightened restrictions on hand guns and fully automatic weapons. The new rules had very little impact on the average deer or duck hunter, but the radio hotliners and right-wing editorial pundits had convinced many people that outright confiscation was just around the corner.

Against this background of inflamed public opinion in my riding, there was no more hope of my winning than there was of Trudeau being awarded the Royal Canadian Legion medal for his contribution to the war effort in World War II. We were dead before we started, and I had told the PM that's how it was when the cabinet had gathered for a retreat at Meech Lake in the summer of 1978.

My participation in that session ended up in the news, courtesy of a leak from one of my colleagues—I don't know who. Soon after I got home from the think-tank session at Meech, I found CTV's Norm Fetterly on my doorstep, asking me if I had truly burst into tears while telling Trudeau that he was electorally killing us. I wouldn't respond then—cabinet discussions are supposed to be confidential—but the answer is "no." Like every minister seated around the oval of tables in the great conference room whose windows overlooked the lake, I was asked to report on the state of things in the six BC Interior ridings for which I was responsible. I told Pierre that a few months before, when the government had been riding high after the election of René Levesque's Parti Québecois in la belle province, we could have won all six. But in the summer of 1978, we wouldn't have won any, including my own.

There were no tears. If I had been tempted to cry, the image of my father would have sprung into my mind, saying, "Don't make a fool of yourself," and that would have dried me up pretty fast. Stoicism is very much an Okanagan trait. We don't cry, and though it goes against the touchy-feely-huggy trend in today's mainstream society, our stoicism is probably a good thing: when you think of what we've had to endure since the first gold hunters came into the Cariboo 140 years ago, we would have done so much crying that we wouldn't have had time for anything else.

So I was not overtly emotional on that February day in 1979 when Lori and I went to tell Pierre that I didn't want to run again. He said he was disappointed, but that it was up to me to decide, and that he would respect whatever decision I made. He asked me for only one concession, before I made an irrevocable choice: that I should talk with Senator Keith Davey, "the Rainmaker" strategist behind the successful Liberal campaign of 1974. Although I thought I had already made an irrevocable choice, and had come to 24 Sussex just to give the PM plenty of warning, I left having committed myself to what I was sure would be an uncomfortable conversation.

I often sat next to Keith Davey in the last row of the caucus during the regular Wednesday morning meetings in Room 308 of the West Block. I took my seat this time with a little trepidation, leaned over and told him that I didn't want to run again and that the boss had asked me to discuss it with him. I'm sure that Pierre had already spoken to the senator and told him to expect me, but Davey—ever the grand showman first feigned complete surprise then blew up like those World War I munitions ships in Halifax harbour. He swore that neither the party nor the government could get along without me, then he showered me with accolades and twisted my arm with a full range of you-can't-let-the-team-downs. I was such a good MP. I was such a good party man.

I had had no idea I was so indispensable. The truth was, of course, that the wily old senator knew exactly which of my buttons to press. I have always been a team player. I believe that we get where we're going because we're going there together. And maybe it's because I was raised on a Catholic reserve and taught by nuns, but I can be a sucker for a well-orchestrated guilt trip. Which is exactly what I got that February. Keith Davey was only the opening act. I began to receive phone calls from caucus and cabinet colleagues, asking me to please hang in there.

So I did. I had planned to tell Pierre then head on back to the riding and inform my campaign core group before any leaks reached them. Instead, I had to tell my family that we were going once more into no-man's-land, and this time we probably weren't going to be coming out in a victory parade. Donna said, "Win or lose we can do it again. It's part of the life when you're in politics."

Somebody once told me that at the Battle of Waterloo, there was a regiment of Irish guards who were sent to occupy a particular place in the line where they were exposed to terrible cannon fire from the French guns. As the day wore on, the regiment received no orders to advance; nor could they retreat because if that part of the field was left empty, Napoleon would have broken through and won the day. So the job of those soldiers, on that day, was just to stand there and take it. And there are days in politics when that's what the job requires.

I remember watching Gene Whelan one afternoon out in front of the Peace Tower when a large and angry mob of Québec dairy farmers came to protest against their not receiving as much of a subsidy as they wanted. "I am *your* Minister of Agriculture," Gene told them, just before they pelted him with a barrage of butter and sour milk. Gene knew what his job required him to do that day. He stood there and he took it.

There were a lot of those days during the campaign of 1979. The Tories had a lock on the riding from the start; they could have run a fencepost with hair on it, and it would have won. I don't want to unjustly disparage Don Cameron, the man who replaced me. But not long after his nomination, he was reported by some of our Liberal supporters to be doing some pre-campaign door-knocking in Merritt—which would have been a sensible use of his time if Merritt hadn't by then been removed from the riding by the 1978 redistribution. Perhaps it's enough to note that nine months after he was elected, his political career was over.

As far as our campaign was concerned, nothing went terribly wrong, but that wasn't enough. Early on, Donna was coming home to the Kamloops house we were living in for the duration, a place loaned to us by our friends Bob and Shirley Gray, who had gone off on a trip around the world. Donna was driving a big Ford recreational vehicle we had rented for the campaign, and hadn't yet gauged the actual height of the thing relative to the Grays' carport. She looked at the resulting damage and said, "There's probably a message in here somewhere."

There was no mistaking the message on the doorsteps. One day, I went door-knocking in Westsyde, a part of Kamloops that's full of modest homes inhabited by the kind of people you could fairly call the salt of the earth. In 1974, just about every door I knocked on had opened to reveal somebody who was going to vote for me. In 1979, it was a shut out. Time and again, it was: "We like you, Len, but..."

Some views were stronger. A man in Chase ran me off his doorstep over the gun control bill. And the most memorable line of the campaign was delivered by a logger named Roy Unterschultz, who was standing in his front yard as I went door-knocking through Vavenby. "Time for the little Indian to go back to the reserve," he called out. And it was.

It was a painful process, but that's democracy. The people are always right, even when you may think they are wrong. I didn't like being—as I think I sometimes was—the available target on which people unloaded their anger against all the social and economic disruptions of the unsettling decade we had all come through since 1968. But now that it's no longer my turn in the barrel, I wouldn't mind seeing the Canadian people get more angry, more often. We don't get mad enough in this country about some of the things that need changing: like the Senate of which I was a member for almost fifteen years—but that's a topic for the next chapter.

On election night, Donna and I drove to the Bavarian Inn in Kamloops to await the results. I'd already heard from party sources back east how badly things were going for us. By the time the Prairies results started coming in, we knew it was a massacre; in the end, we won only one British Columbia seat, that of former Vancouver mayor Art Phillips making his brief foray into federal politics.

In Kamloops-Shuswap, we didn't have to wait for Salmon Arm to weigh in. The earliest polls told us what we had expected to hear. I got up and gave the obligatory, but nonetheless heartfelt, speech to the old gang who had stood by me all through the years. We had done our best, and our best had been pretty good. I found no fault in my campaign staff—I had had as good a team as anybody's, but then I hear that the *Titanic* also had a crack crew.

Jack Dunlop had been our campaign chair, an experienced, hard working political veteran, and he did all that could be done and probably more. For years afterward, whenever we met he would try to take the blame for the defeat—"My fault, Len," he would say—but it was nobody's fault. The people had decided they wanted a change. There were tears all over the place, and a lot of people said things that touched me that night. The one that most surprised me was the declaration by CBC Vancouver cameraman Roy Leblanc that he had specifically asked to cover my campaign that night because he had been sure that I would win. I was sorry to disappoint him.

As Yogi Berra might have said, when it's over, it's over. I was picked up the next day by a government JetStar that Ron Basford had signed out. We stopped in Calgary to pick up Jack Horner and an accompanying bottle of Johnny Walker Red Label, which enhanced the fine dinner we had on the plane. Poor Jack had jumped from Joe Clark's caucus and crossed the floor to become one of us. When I was piloting the metric conversion legislation through the House—if it had been widely known in the riding that I was the minister responsible for metric, I would have lost by an even larger margin—Jack had come to me and implored me not to do away with the acre. "We've got to give the farmers something," he had told me. And so the acre remained the standard unit for measuring farmland, until the Mulroney Conservatives later sent it the way of the rod and furlong.

The last cabinet meeting was brief and businesslike, if perhaps a little more subdued than usual. Trudeau wished us all well; we shook hands and we were gone. I cleaned out my office in the Confederation Building so that Ray Hnatyshyn could take it over. John Fraser of Vancouver South took over the Environment department, which allowed me at least the comfort of knowing it was in good hands. A couple of days after moving out of my office, I realized that I had left something behind and went to get it. The new occupant's staff were brusque almost to the point of rudeness: "Too bad, that's all gone," was how it was put. It didn't occur to me then to think that if the Canadian people had branded our government as arrogant, Brian Mulroney would acquaint them with a whole new class of haughtiness.

Now it was time to find a job. I couldn't go back to science. I was fourteen years behind on the literature, and forty-six was a little old to be shooting for a PhD. There were plenty of smart young men and women who would be rightly ahead of me in the queue for research jobs. So I looked around to see what else might be available.

I had already received a telegram from an old friend, Chief Gordon Antoine of the Coldwater Band down around Merritt. He was the chair of an organization called the Nicola Valley Indian Administration (NVIA), which had been set up a few years previously by the five bands in the Nicola Valley: the Upper Nicola Band, Lower Nicola Band, Coldwater Band, Nooaitch Band and Shackan Bands. Into the NVIA the Indians of the Nicola Valley—named for Nkwala, the last great chief of the Okanagans—had pooled their resources, prorating their shares of the joint venture according to a formula that reflected the size of each band's population: 3, 3, 2, 1 and 1. Although individual band councils still existed, the NVIA looked after centralized health, welfare and education services, and undertook joint economic development projects that would have been beyond the reach of any one band.

Just as I came onto the job market, the NVIA found itself without a chief administrator. Chief Gordon Antoine had wired me to let me know the job was open. But I didn't jump at the implied offer. Although I liked the idea of going home and being among my own people again, I was also very conscious that there could be drawbacks. Many reserves are riven by petty jealousies and family feuds. Some of our people have long memories and a talent for revenge. My family had almost been the victims of such infighting when I was a boy—we had almost lost our land when unfriendly forces had sought to drive us off the reserve.

Besides that, although I had always had the support of most leaders among Interior Indians—including the chiefs of the five Nicola Valley bands, Gordon Antoine, Percy Joe, Don Moses, George Saddleman and Michael Shackelly—not everybody was ready to welcome the lobster back into the bucket. I was still hurting from the many cheap shots I had endured as an MP, even though none had come from the Nicola Valley Indians. So before I would give the NVIA serious consideration, I would look around.

A neighbour who was in banking set me up with an interview at the Bank of Nova Scotia headquarters in Toronto. The bank was looking for a consultant to advise on aboriginal banking, but they were only offering $38,000 a year. I couldn't live in Toronto and put the kids through school on that kind of money. I looked at a few other possibilities, but ex-Liberal ministers were a glut on the market that year, and finally I said yes to the NVIA. They were offering $2,000 a month, which may not sound like much, but it was on-reserve work and therefore tax free. And if I did well, Gordon assured me, the salary would go up.

We moved back to Kamloops. The NVIA was in Merritt—as a rookie MP, I had driven the first nail on the "under construction" sign on their downtown headquarters—but we liked the idea of Lori and Len finishing school in Kamloops, where there were more facilities and they had friends. It was a fifty-mile daily commute, but I came to enjoy the drive. I was back in my ancestral landscape, and in the spring especially I loved seeing the birds and wildlife along the way. I would sometimes stop and watch the ducks and swans in the ponds beside the highway. It also put a kind of insulating time between home and the job, which I needed after all those years in the political pressure cooker.

So the years at the NVIA were happy ones. If there were people muttering about my being an apple, they did it in the background where I never heard it. I was home and it was good to be there, and there were some accomplishments I can look back at with pride.

We established a construction company to build housing on the reserves, with a training program that supplemented the local supply of Indian journeymen in the building trades. We created the Nicola Valley Computer Company, which hired and trained young Indians in business skills and handled all the accounting for the increasingly sophisticated operations of the NVIA and the five bands. We helped the two ranching operations, the Upper Nicola Band's Spahomin Cattle Company and the Lower Nicola Band's Shulus Cattle Company, to grow and prosper. As much as possible, we hired and trained Indians for the jobs these business enterprises created and to deliver the centralized social and health services the NVIA provided to members of the five bands. But we did not let a commitment to affirmative action affect the quality of those services: if no qualified Indian was available, we hired non-natives. We also bought 180 acres of undeveloped land behind the Grasslands Hotel in Merritt, from Don McConachie, son of Canadian Airlines founder Grant McConachie. After the Coquihalla Highway came through, the NVIA also bought the hotel and sold the property for a good profit—which proves that Indians can be good capitalists.

There were two achievements I was most proud of during my years with the NVIA. The first was the recovery of the Bevan Ranch, which was yet another stretch of prime land that had been taken from our people when the reserves were allocated back in the nineteenth century. The Bevan Ranch lay right beside the Shulus Reserve, and was clearly ancestral territory of the Shulus Band: they had been burying their dead on it for generations, and it had remained the people's burial grounds all through 20th century, although the Shulus people had to ask permission of the Bevan family every time they wanted to bury their loved ones next to their ancestors.

To his credit, however, when Ron Bevan neared retirement and decided to sell in 1982, he chose to give the Shulus Band first refusal. The band had some money it could put toward the purchase, but not enough—they were about $250,000 short of the asking price. We went to Fred Walchli, the Regional Director General of DIAND in BC—and to my mind, the best who ever served in that capacity—and he helped us take it to the minister, John Munro. Munro and Walchli knew how to find funds in a departmental budget, and they went to work for us. The money came, the ranch was bought. There was no great ceremony about it—as I say, we are a stoical people—but for the first time in a century, the Shulus people could visit the graves of their forebears without having to beg permission of a white man. You'd better believe that meant something to all of us.

The other project I'm proud of was not connected to the NVIA, although I was grateful that my employers gave me time off to see it through. I was asked to join the board of the Round Lake drug and alcohol treatment centre, which had been operating as best it could for several years out of some beat up old trailers. I was also being gently but steadily pressured by my cousin, Emery Louis, and by Graden

Alexis, a councillor of my own band at the Head of the Lake, to chair the centre's building committee. I resisted at first because I thought it would be better for someone else to get the experience, but Emery and Graden knew as well as Keith Davey how to reset my controls, and they eventually talked me into it.

My participation was the NVIA's contribution to the project, and I fell to it with a will. Drug abuse and alcoholism have been a curse to my people. The counsellors at the Round Lake Centre were trying their best to help, but the rough-and-ready facilities offered by their trailers limited their effectiveness. The place was just too depressing, and I was sure we could do better.

I went to Monique Begin, who was Minister of Health and Welfare now that the Liberals were back in power, and started the wheels rolling. In my MP days, I had developed good contacts at Canada Mortgage and Housing Corporation, so I was able to arrange a mortgage. And a good friend was working with the provincial government, so we were able to pull in funding and other door-opening assistance from Victoria. The long and short of it was that we raised about $3.6 million and got the job done. I didn't take a nickel for my work.

In 1983, we opened the new, 36-bed treatment facility at Round Lake. Since then, hundreds of people have gone through it, receiving a unique blended therapy, a holistic approach to healing the body and the spirit that combines sweat lodges and healing circles with psychological counselling. Elders come in to offer traditional counselling, and many of the professionally accredited staff are Indians. The fifty per cent success rate is very good, considering the often horrendous conditions from which the clients come, and to which they return after treatment.

With projects like Round Lake and several others—I was on the board of the Western Indian Agriculture Corporation—the time I spent with the NVIA was busy and absorbing. It has always been important to me to feel useful, and I felt that I was doing good work for my people. But I was not completely divorced from politics in those years. I

Official Opening of a 36 bed drug and alcohol treatment centre at Round Lake on the Okanagan Reserve near Vernon, B.C. May 1983. Johnnie Dick Billy, my old friend from residential school days, was emcee.

paid attention to what was going on around me, and kept in touch with many old colleagues—including Pierre Trudeau who had been returned to office after a nine-month hiatus that ended when Joe Clark made a mathematical miscalculation to rival that of Christopher Columbus.

When Trudeau moved to patriate the Constitution, I was as interested as only a person who began life as a non-person could be. And when I read Section 35 of the document, I was delighted. It enshrined aboriginal rights in the fundamental law of our country, keeping the special connection to the Crown that had begun with George II's Royal Proclamation of 1763. I have already noted that getting the federal vote was the most important legislative action affecting our people in my lifetime; the inclusion of Section 35 was the most important constitutional action in over two centuries. I give credit to its original drafter, the scholar and Liberal Member of Parliament from Vancouver Quadra, Dr. Ted McWhinney. I would also like the record to show that it was Joe Dion of the Indian Association of Alberta who retained Ted to write that draft so that the Association could offer it to Ottawa during the consultation phase.

Chief Frank Calder of the Nisga'a was horrified by Section 35, however, because it enshrined our people's rights without specifically defining them. "An empty box," was how he described it. We argued the issue a number of times because to me it seemed a very full box and a wonderful thing for all aboriginal people. I think history has now come to support my side of the argument, with the Nisga'a Treaty being constitutionally protected under Section 35. Gordon Campbell, the leader of the provincial Liberal Party in BC has challenged that feature of the Treaty in a court case, contending that it amounts to an amendment of the Constitution of Canada. His action has been roundly seconded by Mel Smith, but I'm not aware of any other constitutional experts coming to their camp. It does seem to me that, if the Nisga'a Treaty was a *de facto* amendment to the Constitution, that fact would have caught the attention of the constitutional advisers to the provincial governments, at least one of which would have blown the whistle. So far, the only whistling I have heard has come from Mr. Campbell and Mr. Smith, and it sounds to me like the proverbial whistling past the graveyard.

After the Constitution was signed into law by the Queen, I visited Pierre Trudeau in Ottawa. I went to tell him how pleased I was with Section 35, and with the seven provinces and fifty per cent of the population amending formula that came with the new basic law. I believe that his role in bringing about those accomplishments, along with the Charter of Rights, will someday ensure Pierre Trudeau his rightful place as the greatest prime minister of the 20th century.

But I had another reason to see Pierre. My old caucus colleague Guy Williams had retired, creating a vacancy in the Senate seats from British Columbia. I had heard through the grapevine that I was being considered for the post—indeed, some former staff and supporters

Pierre Trudeau during a 1980 campaign stop for Mack Bryson in Kamloops. The buckskin gloves were made by Charlotte Joe (nee Moses) of Shulus.

were talking about mounting a lobbying effort to advance my prospects of being chosen. Although I told people they were welcome to write letters if they were moved to do so, I discouraged any kind of strident campaign—the decision was Trudeau's, and I had never known him to be swayed by attempts to twist his arm. It was under his Prime Ministership—and during Ron Basford's term as justice minister—that politically-connected lawyers were firmly made to understand that the one sure way to be dropped from consideration for a federal appointment to the judiciary in Canada was to let it be known that you wanted to be a judge.

I told the PM that if he wanted to put me in the Senate, I would accept the appointment. If he didn't want to, I could live with that, too. He said he appreciated my candor and that was the last I heard on the subject for almost two years.

Some people in my former riding were exposed in 1984 to a demonstration of Pierre Trudeau's candor, during the infamous incident of the "Salmon Arm Salute." Again, blame for the event was laid at the door of Trudeau's supposed arrogance, but once again the context was forgotten.

The PM was on his own time, taking his kids on a vacation. For comfort and security's sake they were travelling in a private rail car attached to a regularly scheduled CP Rail train, which was scheduled to pass the Salmon Arm station at six in the morning. The NDP heard about it, probably through one of the rail workers' unions and arranged for a raucous reception on the station platform. So Pierre and his kids were woken up early in the morning on a day off so that he could be treated to catcalls and insults from a standard NDP rent-a-crowd. Under the circumstances, I found his one-fingered reaction to be understandable. Many of us would probably do the same thing under that kind of provocation.

I continued to take an interest in Liberal affairs and became seriously involved in 1984 when Trudeau announced that he would step down as leader. Of course, my friend Jean Chrétien put his name into contention, and I let him know he would have my support. Ross Fitzpatrick, who was by then in Vancouver, from where he was developing a gold mining venture in California's Mojave desert, was deeply involved on Jean's behalf, and the two of us were asked if we would co-chair our friend's leadership campaign in British Columbia.

The Chrétien leadership bid cut across the unwritten Liberal tradition of alternating between francophones and anglophones in the choice of who would head the party. Being by birth what they call in Québec an allophone—my mother tongue is Okanagan—I never thought much of this back-and-forth business. Jean Chrétien had the talents, skills and experience to be a good prime minister—as he has shown himself to be since 1993—and to disbar such a great candidate because of the franco-anglo alternation seemed to me to be one of those foolish consistencies that ought to be done away with.

Besides, I did not think much of John Turner as a potential prime minister. As I've already made clear, I see politics as a team sport. You don't let your side down just because things are not going the way you personally would prefer them to. And sometimes, political life requires you to square your shoulders and just stand there and take it. In the fall of 1975, John Turner was offered a test of whether or not he had those qualities. In my opinion, he failed the test.

Back then, in early September, Parliament Hill was flooded with rumours that he was giving up the finance portfolio and his seat to return to the corporate world. I was worried about what his quitting would do to the government, so I went to see him in his West Block office. It turned out that the grapevine hadn't kept up with the speed of Turner's moves. He was well beyond planning to leave. I found him already cleaning out his files after having been to the PM to hand in his resignation.

Nonetheless, I pleaded with him not to leave. I reminded him that he had been a good minister in the justice and finance portfolios, and said, "We need you on the team." But he fobbed me off with bland platitudes. It was plain that he still wanted to be leader, that he doubted he could ever position himself for the job if he stayed in Pierre Trudeau's shadow. For his own self-interest, I believe, he was going back to corporate Toronto until the time was right to make his move. His resignation's effects on the government and the party were not enough to hold him where we needed him.

A number of people within the party felt the same way, and it was a bitter campaign, though all leadership contests are divisive. I did a lot of phoning and talking and arguing on Jean Chrétien's behalf. But it was all uphill. The party brass had convinced themselves that Turner had the "royal jelly" that would win us votes. The alternation between French and English was also continually stressed. I liked it that he had come back to Vancouver to run—we need more Prime Ministers from BC, or at least ones that last longer—but the charisma John Turner had had when he was dancing with Princess Margaret had been left behind in the corporate suites of Bay Street. The best that could be said of him was that, after nine years away from the game, he had rusted.

As I expected, Brian Mulroney pounded us Liberals into the ground, and the Tories won the largest majority in Canadian history. I had dreaded a Conservative win. I figured that all progress on Indian issues—and there had been a lot of it under John Munro, whom many of my people consider to be the best Minister of Indian Affairs in recent years—would come to a halt. But Mulroney delivered a pleasant surprise: he picked up the Inuvialuit land settlement agreement that John Munro had been working on and saw it through to completion. He kept the Nunavut process going, settled with the Métis in the Northwest Territories and passed the Yukon umbrella agreement. He and Mike Harcourt started the treaty process in British Columbia, but that is a topic for the next chapter.

On June 28, 1984, I was on Seabird Island in the Fraser River near Agassiz, for a board meeting of the Western Indian Agriculture Corporation (WIAC). Back in my MP days, I had lobbied to help establish WIAC, to fill a gap in the lives of Indian farmers. Indians are always conscious of being under federal jurisdiction—we tend to fear involvement with the provinces, because they owe us no respect—so our farmers do not have much contact with provincial agricultural programs. WIAC was created to enhance productivity among Indian farmers by bringing them the kind of expert advice and assistance that non-Indians get from provincial agricultural agents. It staged successful fall fairs, lobbied for farm credit programs, helped form clubs for the study and practice of traditional crafts, and provided an entry for young Indians into the 4-H movement—at times, WIAC involved up to a hundred Indian boys and girl in 4-H beef clubs.

In the middle of the meeting, I received a note from the reception desk saying Donna had called to say that Pierre Trudeau was trying to reach me, and would I please call him back. I left the meeting and called the Prime Minister from an empty office. Pierre came on the line right away, and said, "I'm sorry that I haven't left you much time to think about it, but do you still want to be a senator?" I told him I didn't need any time, and that my answer was what it had been in

1982: if he offered it, I would take it. He did, and I did. The appointment went through that day, and then on the next—June 29—Pierre Trudeau resigned and left public life.

I hung up the phone and went back to the WIAC board meeting. "I'm the new senator," I said. Soon after, they threw a huge going-away party for me in Abbotsford; something like four hundred people came from all over BC to see me off.

I have to admit, I felt a little uncertain about the propriety of joining an unelected body. I had never liked the Senate's sometimes undeserved reputation for indolence, and I did not want anyone to form the impression that I had accepted a sinecure; I had never received an unearned paycheque in my life, and I wasn't going to start now. I was still relatively young and vigorous, and I resolved to throw myself at whatever work they offered me.

It was nineteen years since I had gone off to Ottawa as a minister's assistant to do what I could for my people. There was still plenty yet to do, and I meant to do as much as I could.

CHAPTER 7

Righting Some Old Wrongs

T he Senate of Canada is a basically good idea that has not been properly executed. Old Sir John A. and the other fathers of our country were groping for a mechanism that would restrain any excessive enthusiasm among the people's elected representatives, even though it would be eighteen years after Confederation before Canada accepted the principle of one-man-one-vote and let men who did not own a certain amount of property onto the voters list. An upper chamber composed of persons of means—senators are still required to own at least $3,000 worth of land, which would have been a lot of money in 1867—would provide an opportunity for "sober second thought" in the event that the Members of the House of Commons got carried away and passed a bad law.

I believe that it is still a good idea. There can be such a thing as a tyranny of the majority in a democracy; the treatment of my people by a society that simply brushed aside our rights might serve as a classic example. But the true value of having a bicameral parliamentary system in Canada has never been realized because the Senate has always been peopled by unelected appointees of successive prime ministers. Many of them have been exceptionally able parliamentarians, like Paul Martin Sr., and the wily old Allan MacEachen; but there have been some—and I name no names—who have abused the dignity of their office by taking its salary and perquisites while shirking its duties.

I applaud the efforts of western Canadians to create the Triple-E

Senate, and I disagree with my old friend Gordon Gibson who wrote in the *Globe and Mail* in 1999 that the Triple-E was an idea "whose time has come and gone." Making the Senate into an effective, elected and equal second chamber would go a long way toward ending the imbalances that outrage many westerners and alienate them from the folks back east. If it were up to me, I would reform the Senate by making it an elected body with six senators from each province and one from each territory, perhaps with fixed terms of six years. I would do away with the ridiculous historical anomaly that gives Québec and Ontario twenty-four seats each, while we British Columbians have only six—although I can't see why Prince Edward Island should continue to have four senators for a population of 125,000 people, which is not much more than the combined populations of Kamloops and Merritt; I would probably give them two.

Official Senate photo 1994.

However, in the summer of 1984, I was not entering the Senate to reform it. I was again the willing horse, ready to do some work. But it took me some time to get a grip on just what I was supposed to do. The old habits of a good constituency MP reasserted themselves once I was back on Parliament Hill. I started taking on the kinds of advocacy and problem solving for individuals that had been standard operating procedure when I had been a member of the other chamber. But the Senate is not set up to enable its members to undertake those kinds of duties. I had one staffer to help me and no constituency office. I soon found that I had cut myself too big a slice to swallow: I was trying to chase a dozen files through the bureaucracy without the full-time expert help the job requires. After a couple of months, I realized that I was just wearing myself out and not doing much good for the people who needed help, so I started shunting them toward their MPs, who were better equipped to do the job.

I concentrated on my work as a legislator—that business of sober second thought—reviewing bills that came up from a Commons that was soon in the hands of Brian Mulroney's Conservatives. I did not expect the new government to do much for Canada's aboriginal peoples. The Conservatives under John Diefenbaker had given us the vote, but Brian Mulroney is no John Diefenbaker, as I am sure he would agree. Yet I have to say that I was very pleasantly surprised by the way the Tories carried on some of the work that had been in the Liberal pipe under John Munro's direction as Minister of Indian Affairs and Northern Development, such as the Inuvialuit land claims settlement in the Northwest Territories, and the legislation that gave self-government to the Sechelt Band.

For a senator who wants to earn his keep, there is always plenty of committee work, and I threw myself into it. I joined the Standing Senate Committee on Agriculture right away, and I would have joined the Indian Affairs committee just as quickly, except that there wasn't one to join. The Senate lumped matters relating to aboriginal peoples under the catch-all mandate of a body called the Standing Senate Committee on Social Affairs. I figured that we Indians, Inuit and Métis had been around long enough to rate our own Senate standing committee, and I began to lobby hard to get one established. The key man to convince was Alan MacEachen, who was Leader of the Liberal majority in the Senate, and once I had his backing it didn't take very long before I was the chair of the new Standing Senate Committee on Aboriginal Peoples. We did away with the old parliamentary word "affairs"—it had come to have some slightly tarnished connotations.

Apart from the work, it was good to be back in Ottawa. I had enjoyed the time in Merritt, working with my people again, but I have to admit that I had changed. I was no longer the raw youngster who had arrived in the capital in the summer of 1965. Even after being away for five years, I still felt like an old hand around the Parliament Buildings. I was comfortable in those surroundings, knew where to go and what to do. I saw a lot of familiar faces and reconnected with old friends and colleagues. Donna and I rented a little apartment on Laurier Avenue and slipped back into many of the same social rounds that we had been part of before 1979. With Lori and Len both at the University of British Columbia, we had more freedom than ever before. After a couple of years, we bought a house in the suburb of Orleans, on the east side of the city.

So it was a good life, except for the climate. Sure, fall is beautiful in the Gatineau hills, but the Ottawa winters are just plain horrible. When Mother Nature isn't trying to kill you directly by freezing you solid or burying you in snow, she takes a sly indirect approach and coats everything in ice, so that the moment you walk out onto your driveway, you get dumped on your duff and start sliding downslope into the skidding traffic. And then there are those sultry midsummer days when the temperature heads for forty while the humidity hits 100 per cent: the air is so full of moisture that the sky turns green at the horizon, and you can almost feel the weight of each waterlogged breath hitting the bottom of your lungs.

By 1989, Donna and I had had enough. We bought the house where we still live, overlooking a ravine that runs through the Sahali hills above Kamloops, and I rented a small apartment in Ottawa that I could commute to for work. The building was on an Ottawa boulevard called The Driveway, which ran through affluent areas, and the place's owner kept the outside looking neat enough to prevent the municipal authorities from sending nasty letters. But inside, there

Celebrating 25th wedding anniversaries with our friends Sandy and Ellen McCurrach and Mack and Liz Bryson July 1985.

were some holes in the walls; the floors were neglected and scratched, and it badly needed a paint job. There was no air conditioning in the summer, and in the winter the thermostat often seemed to have an agenda of its own.

But Senators were allowed only $10,300 a year for all expenses incurred in living in the capital, from rent to taxis, which wasn't enough to keep us in luxury. I was not one of those senators who come to the upper chamber after making a fortune in the business world; as an MP, I had never made more than your average middle class salary, and my three years as a minister had not added greatly to our net worth.

So the place on The Driveway was all we could afford. I used to call it my "hole in the wall," and when the *Vancouver Sun's* Barbara Yaffe heard that, she had a photographer shoot the exterior from a flattering angle, then stuck it to me as if I were some effete snob who complained while living in a taxpayer-supported palace. It was the kind of mean little shot that certain reporters are always willing to take, and putting up with them is part of the price you pay for being in politics. But although I don't know the style of Barbara Yaffe's upbringing, I'm willing to bet, just going by the odds, that I have a closer familiarity with the smell and taste of real poverty than she has.

───◆◆◆───

I had not come back to Ottawa with a hard and fast list of personal goals. But once I realized that I would not be immersed in all that time-consuming "constituency work," I set myself to find ways in which I could advance the cause of aboriginal peoples through the mechanisms of the Senate. I think it's fair to say that my people had not been a particular concern of most of my fellow senators, but there were many able and willing people in the Red Chamber, and it was easy to get a good team on the Standing Senate Committee on Aboriginal Peoples, of which I was the chair. Now I had a mechanism for enlisting the most valuable, if most consistently underrated, capacity of the Senate—the capacity to bring to bear all of its members' considerable expertise and experience in conducting special studies into issues affecting the common good. I had a few in mind.

But before we got to any of that, in June 1985 I found myself dealing with a bill whose subject directly and painfully touched my family and me. It was Bill C-31, amending the Indian Act; it had been shepherded through the House by the well-meaning Tory Minister of Indian Affairs, David Crombie, and which now came to the Senate for our sober second thoughts. It was a good-intentioned bill, a decent effort to undo a number of horrific injustices that had been laid upon some of our people—especially upon our women—by that all-encompassing federal law which for decades had marked out the length and breadth of our existence.

Bill C-31 dealt with the crucial issue of *identity*—who is an Indian, and who is not? The issue is crucial because the Indian Act singles out certain people, and no others, to be recipients of particular treatment under that law. This is not, as some have maintained—including some who should know better—a singling out on the basis of race. It springs from a recognition, going back to the Royal Proclamation of

1763, that this land was not empty when the Europeans arrived. There were organized human societies here, and the members of those societies were entitled to some minimal consideration of their existence even as those societies were being permanently disrupted. That is why we Indians have always had a different legal status, which was codified about a century ago in the original Indian Act. The Act recognizes not race, but legal status: you can be legally an Indian and be covered by the Indian Act, though you haven't a drop of Indian blood; if you are not legally an Indian, it does not matter what genes you carry—you are not entitled to any of the benefits provided under the Act.

Because the whole Indian Affairs apparatus is founded on legal status, it is fundamentally important to be able to decide who is or isn't a status Indian. So the Indian Act set out some rules, one of the most important of which was 12(1)(b) which related to marriage, and which was founded in the blatant sexism of the late nineteenth century, when women—like Indians—were not legally persons, and were therefore considered to be "of one flesh" with their husbands.

It seems strange to us today, but it all apparently made sense to our grandparents: an Indian woman who married a non-Indian man became, legally, whatever he was—white, Chinese, Japanese—while a non-Indian woman who married an Indian man became, legally, an Indian. I've heard it argued that this part of the Act was intended to prevent white men from gaining control over reserve lands by marrying Indian women, but I don't think there are many examples of whites who wanted choice reserve lands having a lot of trouble convincing the government to cut off big stretches and deliver them on a legal platter.

By the 1960s, with the rise of feminism, the Section 12(1)(b) was looking more and more out of synch with reality. When I was an assistant to Art Laing, an Ojibway woman named Jeanette Corbier Laval, from Wikwemikong Reserve on Manitoulin Island, was fighting through the courts, citing the Canadian Bill of Rights—which had application to federal statutes—in an attempt to regain the status she had lost by marrying a non-Indian. She went all the way to the Supreme Court of Canada, where she lost. Mary Two-Axe Early, a

Mohawk from Kahnewake was another of the early activists, as was my friend Mildred Gottfriedsen, who was president of the BC Native Women's Association, *Chatelaine's* 1964 Mother of the Year, and the first woman of our people to be named to the Order of Canada. Through the 1970s and into the 1980s, the fight to regain lost status became the central issue for Indian women's organizations all over the country.

John Munro had wanted to resolve the issue and had actually passed an Indian Act amendments bill in the Commons by 1984. On the last day before Parliament dissolved for the election, he took it to the Senate to try to get it through the upper chamber. But to get such rapid passage of a bill, the Senate must give unanimous consent to a waiving of the normal procedures, and two Senators—Charlie Watt, an Inuit from northern Québec, and Davey Steuart of Saskatchewan—would not allow such an important matter to go through without debate. So the bill never became law.

I give full credit to David Crombie for trying to do the right thing. He didn't wait but picked up right where John Munro had left off. But the bill that he got through the Commons and brought to the Senate in 1985 was badly flawed. It restored status to Indian women who had married non-Indian men, but in some cases not to their descendants.

The amendments to the Act perpetuated the old injustices, and I felt deeply that the bill had to be amended because it had divided my own family. My wife, Donna, is a fair-skinned, blue-eyed descendant of British immigrants, but by marrying me she became legally an Indian, and our children and grandchildren are Indians. My sister, Pauline, however, was married to a man of Japanese ancestry. She lost her status when she married, regaining it in 1985 when Crombie's amendments were made law. But her grandchildren cannot legally be Indians. Their heritage and their rights have been denied them, and that is wrong.

I have never been one to wear my heart on my sleeve. Anytime I have been tempted to make a public display of emotion, my father's words have come back to me from that day in the tomato field. So I did not make an open fuss about this bill. But I poured my heart out in caucus, pleading with John Turner to get behind the women who had fought so hard for justice and now were being offered this half a loaf. But Turner wouldn't budge. I tried to enlist the aid of some of my Senate colleagues, but the interest just wasn't there. It was something that could be looked at again, down the road sometime, when higher priorities had been seen to.

While the bill was in committee, I phoned Jeanette Corbier Laval to ask her opinion. She gave me the same reaction as Gail Stacey-Moore, a Québec woman who was president of the National Indian Women's Association: it was a bad bill, but for the time being they would take the half a loaf. Again, credit to David Crombie: he knew his bill was flawed, and he agreed to fund court cases for Indian women who wanted to challenge the law. Still, I could not bring myself to vote for his bill. I did nothing, however, to oppose it; I agreed to let it pass through the Senate "on division," that is, it received approval without a formal vote.

It is now more than fifteen years since I agreed not to stand in the way of this half-measure, yet we have apparently still not come far enough "down the road" to reach the point where the injustice to my sister's grandchildren, and to thousands like them, can be made good. Again, I find myself asking, where is the great Liberal Party of Canada? Why are we allowing this matter to worm its way slowly through the courts? We have a majority government, on its second mandate; the deficit is under control and Canadians are at peace with themselves and the world; when will we have time for justice?

But I don't want to just stand and point the finger at Parliament. There is fault on the Indian side, too. I know that there are a lot of good-hearted white people who romanticize our cultures, perpetuating the old myth of the "noble savage" living in harmony with all the universe. But we can be as mean and intolerant as anybody else, and some of those bad attitudes were part of the Indian opposition to the restoration of women's status. Growing up, I heard many a disparaging comment about women who had married non-Indians, about how they had made their beds and would have to lie in them. "You turned your back on us," was how it was often put, "and we don't want you coming around here any more."

Then there is the simple motivation of greed. More people entitled to live on a reserve means more pockets into which band funds must be shared out. People who lost their land along with their status may come back and want their property rights restored, to the discomfort of those who now occupy and use those woods and fields.

Land has always been a big concern to our people. That may be because we get up every morning and look out at a landscape that had once been ours alone since the beginning of time, but which came into the possession of a lot of relative newcomers without our say-so. Or it may be a result of all the years when the only way we could make a living was by farming, and cattle ranching and wood-cutting, when land was the one form of wealth we could get our hands on. And some of us were willing to do whatever it took to get more land, even at our neighbour's expense.

In April 1954, as a young man of twenty, I stood in the back of the community hall on our reserve while a federal Commissioner of Inquiry—a Vernon lawyer named Charles Morrow—heard evidence from my father, his brothers and uncles, as to why they were legitimate members of Okanagan Band Number One. Before I got there, the inquiry had already heard evidence from other members of the band that all us Marchands were really American Indians who were illegally squatting on reserve land that one of us had tricked a late chief's old widow into selling to us. The allegations were bogus—that's how the commissioner ruled—but if the complainants had been successful, the accusers could have ended up with some prime productive land, well worked for years by our family's muscle and sweat.

The allegations were old news in 1954. Previously, the same complainants had charged that we were not any kind of Indians at all, but French-Canadians—because of the name, I suppose. My sister, Pauline, can remember the "Indian doctor" woman who lived up the creek from us spitting on the edge of our lawn to lay a curse on our family. Hatred is not too strong a word to describe how some families felt about other families on our reserve. There was some racism behind it, but it was mostly about greed.

Jealousy and rivalry among families and groups of families are common on reserves. It's probably the same in small agricultural villages of any society in the world, and I guess it just goes to show that we Indians are human, too. Like any other people, sometimes we need the law to protect us from ourselves. While the Commons was debating C-31, I remember a CBC television interview with a Saddle Lake Reserve man named Fred Cardinal, who talked about how matters might have to be settled by "an appeal to Judge Colt"—meaning by the gun.

It was because of those kinds of attitudes and because of my memories of growing up in an atmosphere of family feuds, that I argued that we must not leave the power to determine a returning woman's band membership in the control of band councils. It should be a matter for the Registrar of the Department of Indian Affairs and Northern Development in Ottawa. Otherwise, I knew that money, land, racism and petty rivalries would come into play in many cases, and I wanted the women's rights—and their children's—to be unfettered and protected at the highest level. But I didn't win that argument. I settled for the half a loaf, and a promise that justice would be done later.

But now later is here, and justice has still not been done. And I say, bluntly, that it is a shame on us Liberals, on our party, that just as with the federal vote, we have once again left my people the last in line, waiting for someone to get around to noticing that Indians have not yet received justice. A couple of years ago, I wrote to Jean Chrétien, making the most impassioned case I could for doing the right thing, but I have received only an acknowledgement, not a definitive reply. As I am writing this book, it is the summer of 1999, and Bob Nault, the MP for Kenora-Rainy River, has just replaced Jane Stewart as the Minister of Indian Affairs. He will be hearing from me on this issue. It's not just principle; it's personal.

In 1986 one group of British Columbia Indians, tired of waiting to see what the courts might decide about aboriginal title in the Nisga'a land claim case, decided to take a different approach. The Sechelts, under Chief Stan Dickson and the band council, brought forward their own bill to establish self-government. It was a unique approach that no other band has imitated, but when the question was put in a referendum, ninety-three per cent of the Sechelts voted in favour of taking an unusual route to get out from under the Indian Act.

Under a special Act of Parliament—the Sechelt Self-Government Act—the Indians of the Sunshine Coast gave up their taxation exemptions, had their reserve lands deeded over into fee simple ownership, and generally dropped both the shackles and the protective armour provided by the Indian Act. Ironically, the result was much like what would have happened all over Canada if the 1969 White Paper had ever become the law. The Sechelts became fully participating citizens of Canada, without special status, just like everybody else.

I helped—as much as an opposition senator could—to pilot the bill through Parliament. Members of the Sechelt delegation, like Clarence Joe Jr., whose father had been a good friend to me, used to hang out in my Senate office when they were lobbying on the Hill. But I have to say that I did not like the idea behind the bill. Instead of claiming their rights under Section 35 of the Constitution, the Sechelts were accepting delegated powers established by a vote of Parliament. And, of course, anything bestowed by one Parliament may some day be taken away by another.

Some of the national Indian leadership were not happy with the precedent the Sechelts were setting, but as Assembly of First Nations President George Erasmus said, it was nobody's business but the Sechelts'. It is now more than thirteen years since the Sechelt Self-Government Act was passed, and the final agreements are being put in place, but no other Indian band has come forward to follow their lead. I think the Sechelts have every right to be proud of what they have accomplished. They worked hard on their draft bill, and I guess they're entitled to call the big photo they had taken of Clarence Joe Jr. and the others a portrait of the Fathers of Confederation.

I only wish that the next major encounter between Canada and its original inhabitants could have been as positive. Instead, a stretch of two-lane blacktop on a minor Québec road became the scene of a months-long standoff between armed Mohawk warriors and the Canadian Army.

A decade has now passed since the events of the summer of 1990. For most Canadians, probably the only memory that sticks is that television picture of the imperturbable young Canadian soldier, nose to nose with a Mohawk in combat fatigues. It is a fair image. The Army did what it had to do—it upheld the rule of law—neutrally and without rancor or racism. I don't know of any Indian leader who has a word to say against the conduct of the Canadian forces during that crisis. I guess all that peacekeeping training paid off. Certainly, it would have been a much different business if it had been left in the hands of the Québec Provincial Police, or even the RCMP—many of my people do not consider the Mounties a neutral force, as the later incident at Gustafsen Lake made clear.

But for our people, what sticks in our minds is what caused the trouble in the first place: the attempt by the Mayor and Council of the municipality of Oka to turn a sacred Mohawk burial ground into a golf course. Now, maybe that phrase "sacred burial ground" has become, for the average Canadian, just an empty cliché of "Indianness"—like the Hollywood "leathers and feathers" look that many Indian peoples adopted, instead of the cedar bark cloth or woven blankets that their ancestors really wore. But it is not a meaningless, worn-out phrase to us. The places where our forebears' bones lie are as sacred to most of our people as the Vatican is to a devout Roman Catholic, or as a Clayoquot Sound rain forest is to a Greenpeace activist.

When the Shulus people got the Bevan Ranch back, it was not just a land deal. It meant restoring to a small part of the universe its rightful moral order, and regaining some of the dignity that had been scoured away by generations of disrespect. So when the Mayor and Council of Oka proposed that the Mohawk dead should provide a foundation beneath some pretty lawns where white people in overly bright clothing would traipse around, occasionally smacking a little white ball into a cup beneath a silly little flag, the outrage felt by the descendants of those dead Indians was totally real. Imagine if a bunch of Indians showed up at Lourdes and announced they were going to turn the cathedral into a lacrosse box. I think the local parish would do more than sign petitions. It was a measure of how strongly Indians all over the country felt that my own band, the very conservative Okanagan Head of the Lake Band, went out and set up an information picket on the highway that runs through the reserve.

But, although I understand the outrage, I can't condone violence or even the threat of violence. As Chief Justice Antonio Lamer wrote in his decision on the Delgamuukw case, "We are all here to stay," and we will never learn to live together in harmony if we reserve the right to threaten or attack each other—Kosovo and Ulster are the living proof of that. Besides, the Mohawks at Oka, whether they were ex-Marines or Vietnam vets, could never have done more than make themselves a symbolic sacrifice. My old friend Chief Gordon Antoine's wisdom about counting the guns still applies.

As an opposition senator, I did not have much leverage to influence the Mulroney government's day-to-day response to the crisis, but I did what I could. I pressed Jean Chrétien, who was by then our leader, and the rest of the Liberal caucus to call for a non-violent resolution to the stand-off, but I'm sure the Prime Minister was more affected by public opinion polling than by ineffectual noises from across the Commons aisle. Fortunately, a lot of Canadians supported the Mohawks over the would-be golfers.

One thing I could do, as chair of the Standing Senate Committee on Aboriginal Peoples, was to hold hearings on the whole business. I gavelled the first hearing into session on August 2, 1990, three weeks after Québec police first attacked the barricades, but I have to say that the only thing we Senators could usefully do was to get some of the story onto the public record. We heard testimony from the Kahnasetake elders and from well-known Mohawks like Kahn-Tineta Horn, from Canadian Human Rights Commissioner Max Yalden and AFN President George Erasmus. But the people behind the barricades wouldn't come—they would surely have been arrested—and neither would the ever unavailable Minister of Indian Affairs, Tom Siddon, whom we Indians called "Hidden Siddon," because he was such a hard man to see. We also asked the Mayor of Oka to come before us, but he refused, and we had no power of subpoena.

A few days after the stand-off began, I received a call from Christine Deom, an old friend and a recently graduated law student whom I had helped find a firm with which she could article. Christine's husband was Joe Deom, one of the leaders of the Mohawk militants, and through her I began to keep in touch with the group behind the Oka barricades. I was worried by the depth of the anger and the tendency to despair among the warriors; I knew this could go badly if emotions began to overpower reason, and I continually asked Christine to reassure her husband that we were all searching for a peaceful solution.

I thought we had the opportunity for a happy ending, when we were several weeks into the crisis. Christine phoned with a message from Joe: they would put down their weapons and come out if Brian Mulroney would agree to meet with them. I relayed the request to Jean Chrétien, who passed it on to Paul Tellier, Mulroney's Clerk of the Privy Council. But I heard no response and nothing came of it. I had followed the proper procedure as a good team player, but now I wonder if it might have been better to have told the PM directly, or even to have leaked it to someone like Dennis Trudeau, the CBC television reporter whose coverage of the crisis was so excellent.

For me, as for most Indians in Canada, the Oka confrontation evoked feelings of frustration and helplessness, emotions we have grown used to. I was glad when it ended without bloodshed and with the Mohawks able to walk out with dignity. And though I do not fault the Army for its handling, I was not ready to go along with a proposal to have the Senate vote its thanks to the military. The Commons had already expressed its gratitude when one of my friends in the Senate came and asked me if I would support such a motion. It was Senator Jack Marshall, a World War II veteran and a Jew. I answered him this way: "Jack, if it had been your people behind the razor wire, what would you do?" The motion was never put.

I began this chapter with a brief reminiscence about the property qualifications that were required in 1867 before a man (and it was only men in those days) could vote in elections to Parliament. Those qualifications automatically excluded Indians, since any land we occupied was actually deemed to belong to the Dominion government, as it was then called. And just to make sure no Indians managed to overcome that legal barrier, for most of the first four decades of Canada's existence, there was no national electoral system: Canada used the systems in place in the provinces, and every provincial elections act denied us the franchise.

In the nineteenth century, we were despised as "barbarians" and "savages," not worthy of the vote; in the twentieth century, we were mostly just forgotten. There were some exceptions: Indians could vote while they were serving in the armed forces during the World Wars and the Korean conflict, but accepting the franchise could mean losing your Indian status and your treaty rights. Some returning veterans found themselves barred by the Indian Agent from coming back to their own homes on the reserves—having been enfranchised, they were legally no longer Indians. Inuit were given the vote—on paper, at least—in 1950, but no ballot boxes appeared in their communities until the election of 1962. Indians finally got the vote, with no strings attached, in 1960, but there were still some major invisible barriers that kept us from electing our own Members of Parliament.

In 1991, Brian Mulroney appointed Pierre Lortie to chair a Royal Commission on Electoral Reform. I decided to make a presentation to the commission, as a private citizen, on the issue of aboriginal participation in the federal electoral process. I did some research and demonstrated that although aboriginal peoples made up more than four per cent of the Canadian population, we had nowhere near an equivalent representation in Parliament—and there was scant likelihood that we ever would. We were thinly scattered across the country; except for two seats in the Northwest Territories, there were no ridings where we were the majority. There were some northern ridings below the 60th Parallel where we did form a significant segment of the population, but the north-south axis on which riding boundaries are always drawn in the north would invariably include a city full of non-aboriginals who could outvote us.

In the whole history of Canada, there have been some 11,000 people elected as Members of Parliament. Sixteen of them have been

Indian, Inuit or Métis. With the exception of Louis Riél, I have met every one of them. There has never been an aboriginal Member of Parliament from Ontario, Québec, New Brunswick, Nova Scotia, Prince Edward Island, Newfoundland or the Yukon. Now, you might say, "Well, that's democracy. We all have an equal say, and the majority rules." But it's not true democracy when the majority gets all-or almost all—the seats; there must be some provision for the minority to be heard, to be part of the process. Canada's Supreme Court has determined that "identical treatment" can result in serious inequality, as Anatole France alluded to in his famous line about the majestic equality of the laws of France, which forbade "rich and poor alike" to steal bread and sleep under bridges.

Other countries have found ways to adapt the British parliamentary system so that it can accommodate an aboriginal population that has found itself overwhelmed and at risk of being completely marginalized by the settler society. New Zealand, particularly, has a very successful system. It allows Maori voters two options: to register on the general voters list and cast their ballots for candidates in the constituencies where they live; or to register on a separate Maori voters roll and vote for candidates to fill a certain number of seats in the New Zealand Parliament that are set aside for the indigenous people.

I proposed to the Royal Commission studying our electoral system that Canada should try something along the lines of what New Zealand has done. I recommended that Canada create a number of Aboriginal Electoral Districts, in which voters who register themselves as Indian, Inuit or Métis would be able to vote for aboriginal candidates to represent them in Parliament. The idea caught the interest of the Royal Commission, which gave my researcher, a Métis named Marc LeClair, a contract to study the issue more fully and to come back with a more detailed paper after we had conducted a round of consultations with native leaders throughout Canada.

Our research stirred even more interest at the Royal Commission, which then asked me to bring together a group made up of present and former aboriginal MPs—the Committee for Aboriginal Electoral Reform—to hold hearings across the country. We were a non-partisan group: Jack Anawak, Liberal MP for the eastern arctic riding of

Nunatsiaq; Ethel Blondin, Liberal MP for the Western Arctic; Willie Littlechild, Conservative MP for Wetaskiwin; and Gene Rhéaume, former Tory MP for the Northwest Territories. We would have liked to have had former NDP MP Wally Firth to make it an all-party effort, but he was working for the CBC at Inuvik, and the Corporation would not grant him leave. We spent two months holding hearings in most provinces, getting a very strong response from aboriginal peoples' organizations, band and tribal councils and thoughtful individuals, not to mention the input of notable mainstream political figures like Joe Clark and the editorial boards of major newspapers. We received some good coverage in the media, although some commentators got their neck hair up at the prospect of representation based on race, which immediately conjured up—for them, at least—the spectre of apartheid.

But, again, it's not an issue of race. It's a simple recognition that we were here before any settlers. This was our land until strangers came and set up their own system to govern it, and us—a system that left us outside the door. Because of deliberate, systemic discrimination over generations, coupled with a dedicated governmental and social effort to expunge our ancient cultures, we are today at a significant disadvantage in gaining access to, and results from, the political process. At the same time, because of what was done to our ancestors and to many of us who are still living, we are the people most in need of being well-represented in the places of power. The non-aboriginal people of Canada must not say to us, "You have the vote; that's all you're entitled to." We are no longer called barbarians and savages, but the political deck is still stacked against us.

Our findings were included in Pierre Lortie's recommendations as Royal Commissioner, and I do believe that Brian Mulroney would eventually have moved to give Canada aboriginal electoral districts, if his government had survived. I have no other evidence than his willingness to carry on what John Munro and other Liberal Indian Affairs ministers had begun, as he did with land claims negotiations and the Sechelt self-government agreement. I am disappointed that the present government has not put any of its considerable political capital behind this concept, but some of their lack of interest may reflect the fact that the issue of electoral reform was not a high priority with Ovide Mercredi during his tenure as head of the AFN, nor have I heard Phil Fontaine raise the subject since he took over the leadership.

But I wish this idea's time would come, and soon. It is needed. A dozen or so aboriginal Members of Parliament, conscious of themselves as an aboriginal caucus, could not overturn governments or set the policy process on its ear—but they could be a catalyst for substantial change. At the very least, they would make it more difficult for Canadian politicians, and Canadians in general, to yawn and roll over and forget about us again.

In 1993, Brian Mulroney handed his government to Kim Campbell, who took the Conservatives into an election that whittled them down to only two seats. With the Liberals back in power, the prospects of my getting something done for my people seemed brighter, and in the first post-election caucus of my fellow Liberal Senators I pushed for action on an injustice that had been festering in our community for seventy-five years: the lousy way in which returning aboriginal soldiers had been treated after volunteering for service in the three wars that Canada had fought in the twentieth century. It was agreed that our veterans' grievances would be the first matter to come before the Standing Senate Committee on Aboriginal Peoples when Parliament resumed.

I was no longer to be the chair of the standing committee. There was a movement within the Senate to diminish the atmosphere of partisanship—we were there for sober second thought, after all—so it seemed best to let opposition members chair some of the committees. Aboriginal Peoples was chaired by Senator Raynell Andreychuk, and I was deputy chair.

The treatment handed to discharged aboriginal soldiers after the two World Wars and Korea was a lasting shame upon Canada. Thousands of Indian, Métis and Inuit men and women volunteered to serve—even though many of them were specifically exempted from military service by treaties that went back to colonial times. In nine of the provinces, according to World War I statistics, fully thirty-five per cent of able-bodied Indian and Métis men signed up. They went overseas, they fought in the trenches of Belgium and France, and many of them died there. Many came back with a row of medals—Francis Pegahmagabow, an Ojibway, was one of only 39 Canadian soldiers to be awarded the Military Medal plus the maximum two bars for bravery.

In World War II, Canada's aboriginal people again rallied to the Army; the Air Force and Navy regulations required recruits to be of "pure European descent." Again, despite treaty exemptions, most able-bodied Indian men were in uniform. They fought in the raid on Dieppe, stormed Juno Beach on D-Day, and waded through the Scheldt Estuary's flooded polders under German fire. Tommy Prince, a grandson of the great Saulteaux Chief Peguis, earned the Military Medal and the US Silver Star, pinned on him at Buckingham Palace by King George VI. It was the same in the all-volunteer force that went overseas under UN command in 1949—hundreds of Canadian Indians and Métis served their country on Korea's nameless numbered hills, and many of them never came back.

In all the testimony of aboriginal veterans who came before our committee, I did not hear one complaint about discrimination or unequal treatment within the Canadian Army. Whatever their colour, once they were in uniform, they were all equal—same food, same pay, same hardships, same medals. But when they came home and took off those uniforms, the heroes were suddenly just a bunch of Indians again. The Department of Veterans Affairs had benefits for returning veterans, but most aboriginal soldiers got less than their white comrades, and far too many of them got nothing.

After World War II, there was a Veterans Land Act that provided farmland and a low-interest loan to buy equipment, seed and livestock. But for status Indians, the benefits were filtered through the Indian Agent, who had the power to arbitrarily deny an Indian veteran his rightful due. The only land a status Indian could acquire under the VLA was reserve land, which meant it legally remained under the ownership of the band council, and might be taken back at any time. Many Indian veterans were not informed by their Indian Agents of what they were entitled to. In some cases, it appears likely, from some of the talk at the time, that Indian Agents lined their own pockets with funds that should have gone to ex-soldiers. Although there were many decent men in the Indian Affairs Branch in those times, there were others who did not qualify as the cream of the Canadian civil service.

Métis veterans did not have Indian Agents over them, but many of them went home to remote communities that were no more than a few log cabins at the end of a bush trail. The programs that were advertised to soldiers back from the war through newspapers, radio and the Royal Canadian Legion's newsletter might as well have been posted in Chinese on a bulletin board in Beijing. Most Métis never even heard about them.

Many veterans got their information through word of mouth at the Legion. But status Indians couldn't go into a Legion in 1945—the law prohibited us from entering drinking establishments—and besides, most Legions were in towns and cities, while most Indians and Métis lived a far piece from the nearest concrete sidewalk or streetlight. It was still the same in 1951. Our people had marched shoulder to shoulder with white Canadians in uniform, but once they were home again, all the old barriers went back up.

The Standing Senate Committee on Aboriginal Peoples put professional researchers to work on the old files, but we could not find a single instance of an Indian veteran getting land under the Veterans Land Act. We did find cases of the Dominion government taking Indian land after World War I—73,000 acres from Saskatchewan reserves—and giving it to white veterans. Similar things happened in British Columbia: the Blueberry River and Doig River bands of Cree in northeastern BC lost 18,000 acres, from beneath which eventually came millions of dollars worth of oil and gas. Chief Apsassin hired Tom Berger to go to the Supreme Court of Canada and in 1995, they won compensation for the Crown's failure to fulfil its fiduciary duty.

I think the worst abuse of status Indian veterans was that many of them came out of uniform to find that they were no longer legally Indians. At some point during their time in the Army, someone had handed them a form to sign, perhaps telling them it was a condition of being eligible for overseas service. Thus they had unknowingly made their marks—many of them were illiterate—at the bottom of an application for "enfranchisement," the legal term for the giving up of treaty rights and status under the Indian Act. Many of the men who found that they were no longer Indians had wives and children who also automatically lost their status, and none of them could live on reserve or receive benefits.

It was part of a long-standing Indian Affairs policy to pressure Indians who were judged to be capable of supporting themselves in the white man's world into accepting enfranchisement. The more paternalistic of the Indian Affairs bureaucrats saw nothing wrong in tricking one of us into giving up status—I assume they thought that an Indian who could soldier on equal terms with whites could cope with civilian life just as handily. They didn't reckon on the reality that, while an Indian in uniform was treated like a man, an Indian in blue jeans was treated like just another Indian. Those who lost their status through war-time enfranchisement eventually had it restored in 1985 under David Crombie's Bill C-31. But it had been a long wait.

It was hard to listen to some of the testimony. These were good people, who had put their youth at the service of their country, many of them risking their lives to fight in wars against racists and dictators, only to come home and be treated as second-class citizens—to be ignored, forgotten, and in some cases, actually robbed of their just reward. There was not much we could do, forty and fifty years after the World War II and Korean vets had paid their dues, and nothing for the World War I aboriginal soldiers who had grown old and died before anyone would even listen to their stories. But we did what we could.

In 1996, the Government of Canada established the Aboriginal Veterans Scholarship Trust, to be managed by the National Aboriginal Achievement Foundation in memory of aboriginal veterans—$1.15 million to begin with, but that has since been slightly augmented— for descendants of those Indian, Métis and Inuit veterans. Eligibility for a scholarship is now available to all persons of native ancestry. It does not give back to those who served what cannot be given back, but one of the things our people were fighting for in Flanders and

Holland and Inchon was a better life for their children. And there is nothing more crucial to the advancement of the aboriginal peoples of Canada than the education of our young.

Our veterans are also now receiving their deserved recognition from the nation and from their comrades at the Royal Canadian Legion. Leaders of the National Aboriginal Veterans Association now participate in the Remembrance Day ceremonies at the National War Memorial in Ottawa. And aboriginal veterans were invited to take part in commemorative pilgrimages to the battlefields of Europe and Korea.

I wish we could have done more. I would particularly have liked to see the completion of the national monument to Canada's aboriginal soldiers that Ron Irwin planned for Confederation Park on Elgin Street. And, if I had stayed in the Senate, I would have nudged the government at every opportunity to get on with it. But the moment came when I realized it was time to call it a day— and I can remember the moment exactly.

It was at 5:30 a.m. on a fall day in 1996. The clock radio woke me up so that I could get down to the Kamloops airport and catch a plane to Vancouver so I could transfer to another plane heading to Ottawa. I lay in bed, looking at the ceiling. Donna was stirring and starting to get up, and I put my hand on her shoulder and said, "No. Go back to sleep. I've had enough."

It was thirty-one years since I'd first gone to Ottawa for a temporary assignment with the Minister of Citizenship and Immigration; I'd spent twenty-eight of those years in service to the public and my people, most of them in a city whose climate I did not care for, far from the landscape of my ancestors. I wouldn't want to know how many of those years, in total, had been spent on airplanes. I was pushing sixty-three years old; I was becoming worried about a sleep disorder that seemed to be getting worse, and I had had enough.

I did not catch the plane. I called Jean Chrétien and told him I wanted out. I thought I was giving him plenty of time to fill my Senate seat before the next election, but he twisted my arm and asked me to stay on: he didn't want the vacancy to stir up the same kind of fuss that was happening in Alberta, where Ralph Klein's pro-Reform

Chatting with President Bill Clinton and Prime Minister Jean Chretien after the President's address to a joint session of the Senate and House of Commons, 1995.

Tories had been happy to embarrass the federal Liberals by holding a choose-your-senator plebiscite in tandem with the provincial election.

For the sake of the team, I stayed on until after the election. I cut back on my attendance in Ottawa—my sleep disorder had begun to affect my general health—which left me open to those easily flung media charges that I was an absentee senator, like the one who was apparently retired in Mexico but still collecting a salary. I have never shirked when it came to hard work, but I was getting beyond it now, so I put up with the cheap shots from the *Vancouver Sun* and others. Sometimes, in politics, you just have to stand there and take it.

I resigned my seat in March 1998. To replace me, the Prime Minister appointed D. Ross Fitzpatrick, who had been one of the "best and the brightest" in that Ottawa of long ago. He had been executive assistant to Jack Nicholson when I joined the minister's staff in 1965. Many of my people's views of life lean toward explaining the world in terms of circles, with endings always coming back to beginnings. Perhaps having Ross replace me is some kind of evidence that we really do understand how the universe works.

For Donna, my leaving the Senate was an occasion for mixed feelings. She liked the life of the nation's capital, the fun and the friends. And we are not wealthy—another ten years of a senator's salary would not have been unwelcome. But it's been more than a year now, and it has all worked out. We're in Kamloops with our children and the grandchildren. We are home.

CHAPTER 8

Our Land, Our Voice

A political career doesn't end abruptly—unless you stomp out and slam the door. I keep hearing the echoes from more than three decades in public life: the University College of the Cariboo has awarded me an honourary Doctorate of Laws, which makes up for the PhD in range management that I never went back for. I was honoured to receive the Order of Canada. I was honoured to be thought of as a potential Lieutenant-Governor, though I couldn't take the job.

My phone still rings: reporters wanting my reaction to events that affect my people; active politicians looking to bounce an idea off me; people—especially my own—seeking to make contact with the political apparatus. That doesn't make me a wheeler-dealer; even when I was deep in the political life, I was very leery of anything that smacked of influence peddling. When people would ask me to introduce them to a colleague, I might do so in a phone call, but I would never accompany them to the subsequent meeting. And I would never accept a benefit of any kind—long after I became an old hand in politics, I was always aware that I was representing my people. I didn't want anyone to ever be able to point the finger at me and say, "There, you see, you can't trust an Indian."

I have no regrets about how things turned out. I would do it all again. Sometimes, I wonder what it would have been like to have spent my life in the laboratory and out on the range, poking around in the mysteries of plant ecology. I would have been happy, I'm sure. But, instead, I made my contribution in another field, and I am

On the occasion of receiving an honourary doctorate from University College of the Cariboo with Nancy Greene Raine and Dr. Roger Barnsley, President of U.C.C.

happy with what I was able to achieve. I opened some doors. I broke trail for others who came after me, though it still troubles me deeply that thirty-two years after my first election, I remain the only Indian ever elected to Parliament from Canada's third largest province. There should have been more of us by now. But I think I know why there have not been.

People who are opposed to affirmative action say that it ought to be enough if everybody has an equal opportunity to show what they can do; we should all line up together in the starting blocks and let the laurels go to whoever runs best. It's a nice idea, but it hasn't got much to do with reality. Reality, for Indians, is that the race started centuries ago, but nobody would let us onto the track until just the past little while. Now that we're actually in the running, it may look as if we're pacing along in the same pack as all the other ethnic groups, but the fact is, we're many, many laps behind everybody else.

There is no level playing field for us. We start out in a deep hole, and there is no comparison to the experience of ethnic minorities that emigrated to this country. I don't minimize the sufferings of the Chinese who built the railroads at a cost of one life per mile, or the Ukrainian farmers shivering in their sod houses on the prairies, or the Japanese behind barbed wire in the World War II internment camps. But all of them were living the classic immigrants' struggle, starting at the bottom, despised and rejected, until they could push their way into the mainstream.

That's not how it was for Indians. We weren't just victimized by temporary head taxes or statutory barriers to joining the professions. We spent generations as legal non-persons, wards of a state that was intent on keeping us powerless while our ways of life were systematically broken down and tossed into the dumpster of history. Other groups were kept out of the mainstream society for a generation or two; we were kept in a prison called the Indian Act for more than a century. Other minorities were ignored and left to fend for themselves; we were paternalistically regulated from cradle to grave, and even beyond—an Indian's will is still not legal unless it is approved by Indian Affairs. When you have lived like that, generation upon generation, you build up a kind of historical momentum. You can't stop on a dime and turn ninety degrees onto a new course just because somebody tells you, "You're free to compete now; lots of luck."

Many of us, as individuals, are doing fine. I am so proud of all the young Indians who have got their educations and who are making good lives for themselves, and I am especially proud of the ones who

Donna and I with our son Len Jr. on his Call to the B.C. Bar, May 1995.

return from school to put their abilities at the service of our people. But there are still not enough of us to make a critical mass within the Indian population, the critical mass that will transform us into what we should be, what we will be, maybe twenty or fifty years from now.

As a people, we need time to get ourselves out of the hole we've been kept in for so long. In that spirit, I want to end this book with some recommendations to the powers that rule our lives.

~~~~~~~

I believe that the Treaty Process launched by Brian Mulroney and Mike Harcourt on the Squamish Reserve in 1992 is, though well intentioned, going nowhere fast. We have spent some $125 million on this process so far, and in practical terms we have achieved nothing. It's not just that the issues are complex and require lengthy negotiation; the problem is that our people are not ready to conduct those negotiations. Besides, most of those that I talk with are inherently suspicious: they see the White Paper all over again, and they fear that Ottawa is scheming to dismantle the Indian Act—which has always been our fortress as well as our prison—and hand them over to the province.

There is a better way to do this. For over a century, the most important fact of life for Indians in British Columbia is that we were cheated out of our land. We were not conquered, and most of us signed no treaties or bills of sale. We were just brushed aside while strangers moved in on our ancestral territories and began to use them for their own purposes, without paying us a dime. These days, we see the province setting aside vast stretches of our land for parks and wilderness preserves or licensing the resource rights to multinational corporations. We worry that if we ever do get our land back, it will be stripped bare of anything valuable.

Right now, the most sensible thing that Ottawa and BC could do about the land claims issue in British Columbia is to make an immediate land settlement. Give us back our land—or at least some of it. I propose that each status Indian be awarded 128 acres, as provided for in Treaty Number 8 that settled things in the Peace River country, and that the territory be held as federal reserve lands under Section 91.24 of the Constitution. By my calculations, that would total about six per cent of BC's total land mass, which is not grossly out of proportion to our numbers within the population, especially when you consider that all of the land used to be ours—and might be again if we have to settle this in court, instead of by negotiation.

A land settlement would give our people what we have always lacked: an economic base from which to become self-supporting. If we had a reasonable portion of land, the resources on and under it could be developed to create jobs and sustainable communities. We would no longer have to depend on government for every scrap of sustenance, and over a generation or two we could pull ourselves out of the hole that history stuck us into and be able to deal with the world as true equals. Then we would finally be in a position to sit down with Ottawa and Victoria to talk realistically about our place within Canada and British Columbia.

I recognize that the Delgamuukw decision, in which the Supreme Court of Canada advised governments to resolve the BC land claims issue by negotiation rather than have a settlement imposed by the court, is the most important victory for my people's cause in my life-time. It was in my Senate office that the delegation of Gitksans—led by Elmer Derrick, Don Ryan and Earl Muldon, holder of the heredi-tary Gitksan title Delgamuukw—met to await the Court's decision on a December morning in 1997. When the phone rang with the first word from the Supreme Court next to the Justice Building at the top of Kent Street, the news plunged the group into dismay: the Justices were sending the case down to the BC courts for retrial; it looked as if we were back to square one. But then the full text of the judgment was brought over, and as we read it, shouts of jubilation could be heard echoing down the Senate's sedate corridors. The Court had ruled that aboriginal title was alive and well; it could not be extinguished at the will of the provincial government. Furthermore, the federal and provincial governments were ordered to arrive at a just and fair set-tlement with the Indians of British Columbia.

Seeing the joy on the faces of the delegation as the meaning of that decision sank in—we had won!—was one of the proudest moments of my life. But Delgamuukw did not solve our problems. The Supreme Court opened a door for us, but I don't think we are yet ready to cross the threshold. The Justices advised all of us to find a way to live together, but I don't believe my people are yet in a posi-tion to make decisions on issues of self-government.

That is why I would like Jean Chrétien and whoever leads the next Government of British Columbia to forget about negotiating detailed agreements on self-government and taxation rights. We're not ready for the Sechelt or Nisga'a models, and ninety per cent of our people are too poor to pay taxes anyhow. Instead, the prime minister and premier should appoint federal and provincial ministers who will work on the BC land question full time, and set a five-year deadline to have the issue resolved. During that time, the federal government should buy up any strategically sited lands that come on the market, like the Douglas Lake Ranch that was offered for sale in 1997. Its 67,200 deeded hectares and 135,200 hectares of provincial grazing and forest land would have met the land settlement needs of at least five local bands.

Making a land settlement may sound simplistic—we are constantly told that the Treaty Process involves such complex and intricate issues—but it's the key to any reconciliation between Indians and the rest of society. The radicals wouldn't like it, but that's because they would be holding out for utopia. The lawyers and consultants on both sides of the treaty table would be disappointed, but I think most of us could live with that.

During debate on the Nisga'a Treaty in the summer of 1998, I raised this idea in an op-ed page article in the *Vancouver Sun*, which was reprinted in a number of BC aboriginal newspapers. The response from Indian leaders and grassroots people, was overwhelmingly positive. The Nisga'a Treaty, though it is fine for the Nisga'a people, is not seen to be a template for any other Indian nation in British Columbia. It shows good faith on the part of the two senior governments, and I am proud to have had a role in getting the negotiations launched, but it is a blind alley as far as other treaty talks go.

The Nisga'a have their own needs and priorities, which are not necessarily shared by other Indian peoples in BC. We are not one homogeneous nation, and we have our differences, just like all those different tribes in Europe. If the Germans decide to arrange their affairs in a way that suits them, would anyone assume that the English, the French, the Italians and the Slovaks would automatically copy them?

The fundamental issue is, and always has been, land. By taking over our lands—often by trickery and sharp practice—the settlers removed our ability to provide for ourselves and made us suspicious of their provincial governments. Give us enough land to work with, and we'll begin to be able to look the rest of the world in the eye again, as equals. Let another generation or two build on that foundation. Then we can haggle over all the details of self-government.

Along with a land settlement, I also recommend that the federal government revisit a suggestion I first made as far back as 1980, and which was last seen as part of the Red Book of Liberal policy in the 1993 election: to take all the grants and subsidies that are now earmarked for the economic development of our people, and combine them as capitalization for an Aboriginal Peoples Development Bank. Hire a real-life, experienced banker to head the organization, and let it be run under a philosophy of no more hand-outs, but plenty of practical assistance for aboriginal people—whether they are individuals, companies, co-ops or band councils—who are trying to develop or expand workable, job-creating businesses.

A good model for such an enterprise is the Peace Hills Trust Company, a wholly owned financial entity of the Sampson Band in Hobbema, Alberta, on whose board I was proud to serve for five years. The company started out sixteen years ago with a capitalization of $10 million; it now has $40 million in capitalization, and the number of bad loans on its books is virtually nil. It has branches in all the western provinces, and it shows that Indians can do business in a businesslike way, if the opportunity is there.

<hr />

The second major recommendation I want to make to the government and to my party is to implement the system of aboriginal electoral districts called for in the Lortie Royal Commission on Electoral Reform. Again, there will be those who will make their usual chittering noises about race-based government; oddly, though, I can't recall many of these oh-so-principled critics ever making an equivalent clamour in our favour—apparently the odour of racism only gets up their noses when they're downwind.

But, again, it is not a question of race; it is a question of history. Just as we are, economically, in a hole that took a century or more to dig, we are just as deeply disadvantaged electorally. If Canada is ever to deal with the problems arising from the way we were marginalized when our ancient territories were settled by all the others who came and stayed, we must look beyond sophomoric simplifications about how our electoral system should work.

Canada manages to survive with an asymmetrical Senate that gives four times as many seats to Ontario as to British Columbia. We reserve four seats in both the Senate and the House of Commons for an island province with a smaller population than a decent sized suburb, yet no one accuses Prince Edward Islanders of taking an over-rich slice of the national pie. If our democracy can flourish in the presence of such imbalance, I am sure it can withstand the strain of welcoming a dozen more Indians, Inuit and Métis into the House of Commons—at least for fifty years or so, until we have got up off our knees and can stand on an equal footing with every other Canadian.

I will make this recommendation any time I am asked, and probably a few times when no one has requested it. In the new century, I want to see more of my people sitting around those tables where the big decisions are made. I wish I could hear the motion being second-ed by leaders like Ovide Mercredi and Phil Fontaine. Perhaps they should go and talk with the Maoris. An aboriginal can and will be Prime Minister of Canada in the twenty-first century.

My third recommendation is that Ottawa must undo the injustice that was done to the children of Indian women who lost, then regained, their status under the Indian Act. We all knew that Bill C-31 was flawed when it was passed in 1985. We knew that families would be divided, that children would be dispossessed of their heritage by a bad law. It was wrong then, it is wrong now and it is past time that we did the right thing. I have written to the Minister of Indian Affairs and Northern Development, Bob Nault, whom I know as a decent man and knowledgeable about native issues. I will continue to speak out about this matter, as long as I have breath, or until justice is done.

I have one last recommendation, not to government, but to any young Indian, Inuit or Métis looking at the words on this page. I say this with all my heart and soul: get every bit of education you can. Whatever you do, stay in school as long as possible. Learn, because learning is power; it is how you come to have choices about what you will do and where you will go; it is how you become free.

Try as much as you can to hold onto your language and culture, but don't spend your life looking back at what was or dreaming about what might have been.

With my old friend Don Moses after finally celebrating our birthday together Nov. 16, 1999

The world is yours if you want it. Go out and be a part of it. Be who you are, and be proud of where you come from. You can do amazing things, for yourself, for our country, for our people.

As I write this, it is the fall of 1999. In a few weeks, I will be sixty-six years old. As I look back, I can see where I have broken the trail these many years, the best I could do in my time. But now I also see that there are thousands, tens of thousands, of young Indians—like my children Lori and Len Jr.—who have come up behind me, and they are smart and confident and fearless, and so wonderfully ready and able to carry on.

So now I can sit down beside the trail to rest and to watch the future move on past me.

The End

The Grandchildren (L to R) Caitlin, Miles, Carling, Keegan, Noah, and Erin. May they have a wonderful life.

Index